WOODSTOCK

Bits & Pieces

WOODSTOCK

Bits & Pieces

— A MONTAGE OF WOODSTOCK, ONTARIO
IN TEXT AND PICTURES

TEXT by
ART WILLIAMS

BOOK DESIGN, TYPOGRAPHY and LAYOUT by
EDWARD BAKER

THE BOSTON MILLS PRESS

CORPORATION OF THE

CITY OF WOODSTOCK

The Boston Mills Press
132 Main Street
Erin, Ontario N0B 1T0
TEL: (519) 833-2407
FAX: (519) 833-2195

The publisher wishes to acknowledge the financial assistance
and encouragement of The Canada Council, the Ontario Arts Council
and the Office of the Secretary of State.

ACKNOWLEDGMENTS

This book could never have been published but for the generous assistance accorded us by many citizens of Woodstock and Oxford County. The senior citizens have supplied us with an unlimited amount of picture material (much of which could not be published due to lack of space in this book) as well as bits and pieces of early Woodstock which otherwise would have disappeared in the coming years.

We have gleaned much from back issues of the Sentinel-Review and thank the entire staff for their assistance. The Woodstock Herald and the Times, although defunct for many years have, unknowingly, been very helpful. Publications from reunions, jubilees and church anniversaries have been a source of information as have the "Memoirs of Rev. Farthing" and Lieut. A. M. Fordyce's "History of the Oxford Militia".

Although it is impossible to list by name all those who have assisted us, special mention should be made of the kindnesses rendered us by some: Mrs. E. J. Canfield, historian; Miss Louise Hill, historian; Mrs. Bernadette Smith, museum curator; the Audio-Visual Aids Division, Ontario Hospital; Mr. J. C. Edwards, photographer; and Mr. G. R. "Bud" Case, photographer.

To our patient, understanding and thoughtful wives, who kept us well supplied with coffee and constructive criticism, we say, "Thank you. Without you, the preparation of this book would never have been possible."

PREFACE

The passing years call our senior citizens to their reward and with them go many interesting facts about our community. These are not to be found in history books but are interesting bits and pieces that make up our local heritage. They cover a wide range of subjects from the birth of Old St. Paul's, Woodstock College. The Estelle, Ballad of Birchall, Jo Boyle, George Washington Jones, disaster and humour.

Combined with this is the growth of Woodstock from a "Town Plot" to the enterprising town it is today. First, we look at it as a clearing in the bush and slowly it emerges as a pioneer town of British aristocracy led by Admiral Henry Vansittart. Their presence is still felt as we look at some of the fine old homes that overlook the City.

As this generation slipped away, another rose to take its place and Woodstock became a city. This step forward brought a new era and the man in the street replaced the aristocratic gentleman of yesterday, both at home and on the battlefields of Europe. The fruits of their labours are seen in the growth of the "Industrial City" and the outlook is bright as we enter the second century of Confederation.

The photographs and maps presented are from the original prints or negatives and have not been retouched in any way. This is the first time most of these photographs have been published. It might be interesting for the reader to compare present-day Woodstock with what he finds between these pages.

It has been our desire in this our Centennial year, to gather together some of these highlights and in a small way preserve that precious thing known as our "Canadian Heritage".

Art Williams and Edward Baker

CONTENTS

THE TOWN PLOT

The first white man to view the site of Woodstock was the French explorer, Etienne Brulé. He lived among the Huron Indians for over twenty years during the early seventeenth century and explored the LaTrenche River (now the Thames) to its outlet at Lake St. Clair.

Southern Ontario was the home of the Neutral Indians at that time. Neutral, being the name given to the Atikiwandaronks because they preferred to supply the necessary fundamentals of war to the Iroquois and the Hurons, made from the flint beds they controlled along the shores of Lakes Erie and Huron. Each year they held trade fairs and the neighbouring tribes came to barter for flintstones and corn, in exchange for furs and hides that the Neutrals required for their preservation.

The coming of the British and French saw the Neutrals exterminated. The Europeans supplied the Iroquois and Hurons with modern arms and eventually the Iroquois destroyed all the Neutrals and most of the Hurons. Southwestern Ontario then became the hunting grounds for the Iroquois and no Indian settlements remained. As late as 1920 the site of a Neutral village was located near Norwich proving their existence.

Nearly a century and a half passed before this district was again inhabited. In 1784 Capt. Joseph Brant Thayandanega, the chief of the Six Nations brought his people to Canada and settled on the Six Nations Reserve near Brantford. They came here because they wished to remain loyal to the British crown and the land was given to them in appreciation of their loyalty during the American Revolution. From this site, many travellers left for the west on their journey between Niagara and Detroit.

Some went through to Detroit while others stopped off and claimed, or purchased land from the Indians. One of these men was John Carrol, who erected a cabin along the river north of Beachville in 1784. He was Oxford's first settler.

During the winter of 1792-3 Sir John Graves Simcoe, the first lieutenant-governor of Upper Canada travelled by sleigh to Brant's Ford and then made his way on foot to Detroit. The reason for his trip was to explore the possibilities of a military road being made from Niagara to Detroit as a line of defence, if the republic to the south wished to invade Canada, which he thought they would. This road was laid out and parts of it are still in existence and known as "The Governor's Road". Among other things he was also in search of a more suitable site for the capital as Niagara was too vulnerable to attack. The present site of Woodstock was not an ideal spot but it was considered as a likely spot for a garrison town along the "'Road."

On facing page — Woodstock, as it appeared to an unknown artist in the 1850's. This pencil drawing shows the original Chalmers Church (steeple on the left), the first Methodist Church (centre steeple) and the old Knox Church. Immediately to the right of Knox Church may be seen the tower of the Town Hall, our present City Hall.

10

The spot selected was marked on the survey as "the Town Plot" and the name proposed was Woodstock after his home town in England. During the survey of Oxford County as we know it, several English names were adopted including Blenheim, Blandford and Oxford.

Simcoe was recalled before his plans could be put into effect, therefore his dreams of the future failed to materialize and several to whom he had granted land lost their holdings.

The first settler to settle near the Town Plot was Zacharias Burtch. He, along with his family, arrived in 1800 and erected the first cabin on the present site of Woodstock's Y.M.C.A. The site became known over the years as Burnside Lodge. The Burtch family were the fore-runners of a surge of settlers who took up land in the immediate area. Among those early settlers we find John Hatch, Nathanial Hill, Sr., Francis Babbitt, Messrs. Barraclough, Lamport and Dibble. These set-tlers did not occupy land on the Town Plot but remained in the immediate vicinity of the present fair grounds, except for John Hatch who built at the corner of Victoria and Dundas Streets.

The original Town Plot consisted of land located in the vicinity of Victoria Park, the County buildings and the block bounded by Light, Graham, Hunter and Dundas Sts.

The influx of settlers continued and in 1833, a survey was partially made by Mr. Reinham, a second one was started by Peter Carroll in 1834 and O. Bartley completed the town's survey in 1844.

The first lot was sold to Mary Hallock on April 25, 1836, followed by sales to Rev. Wm. Bettridge, Abraham Sudsworth, Nathanial Hill and Wm. Clark.

The limits of the town still consisted of the Town Plot prior to 1845 when an Act of Parliament extended the limits. They were further extended when in 1860, half of lot 18, concession 1 of Oxford was added to the town.

Signature of Thomas Hornor, 1825. This authentic signature contradicts the spelling commonly used for more than the last one hundred years on Horner's Creek, which was named after this gentleman.

Archibald Burtch, the son of Zacharias was one of the outstand-ing citizens of this period and he gave freely of his time and efforts to make Woodstock flourish. Originally he came from Coopertown, N.Y. where he was born in 1786. The family migrated to Canada in 1799 after accepting an invitation from Lord Simcoe to come and take up land. After a short stay at Brant's Ford they continued on to Hornor's Blenheim settlement, before plunging into the wilderness in search of their new home.

Three days of cutting brush and slashings were necessary as they made their way through the lowland west of Hornor's settlement. The thicket was so solid that the oxen could not force their way through. Archibald Burtch took up the west half of lot 19 and later the other half.

He married a daughter of Squire Teeple and erected a frame dwelling. This was to become the starting place of the Town. His first wife died and he married Jane Blow the same year.

Henry Vansittart, Rear Admiral of the Blue in His Majesty's Royal Navy.

Jane was to become his inspiration and her reputation for energy and zeal in promoting the settlement soon became the topic of conversation when travellers met. Their home became the stopping off place for new arrivals and their hospitality became so taxed that they were forced to open a tavern in self-defence.

Originally the tavern handled spirit refreshments but Mrs. Burtch soon realized the folly of her ways and ceased its sale, but retained a boarding house. During the erection of old St. Paul's Church, she cared for fourteen men on a permanent basis as well as the travellers who continued to arrive. The old home stood until 1852 and the now famous Burtch Home was erected. Archibald died in 1866 and Grandma Burtch went to her reward in 1896 at the age of 92 years.

The railroads were of considerable interest to Burtch who saw them as the leader in trade and commerce. He donated ten acres of land to the Great Western and a right of way through his property to the Port Dover and Lake Huron Railroad when these lines were being promoted locally.

He also had a great interest in education and politics. Once, when the Woodstock College was in need of funds he placed a mortgage on his property to see them through their trying times. He also served on the first county council as a member, and was engaged as clerk, assessor, tax collector for his local council. Politically he was a supporter of the Reform Party and a personal friend of Francis Hincks.

The arrival of Admiral VanSittart and his party was the turning point in the life of Woodstock. Following the Napoleonic Wars in Europe there was a trend to go to the colonies and members of the aristocracy were inclined to believe that they could carry on as they had done at home. They soon recognized their error, and those with the proper spirit endured the hardships while others returned home as soon as possible. VanSittart's ambition was to create homes for his sons but he remained in Canada for the rest of his life.

He sent Capt. Andrew Drew as an advance party to secure land and make the necessary arrangements for his family's arrival. Drew was to arrange for a church, while VanSittart would solicit sufficient funds to endow it.

Capt. Drew arrived in 1832 and purchased considerable land in the east end. The VanSittart party arrived in New York on June 1, 1834 and proceeded to Woodstock. Along the route, the Admiral's wife died but was brought on to Woodstock for burial. VanSittart had included a sailing ship which he hoped to reassemble and sail on the Thames. It is said that when he saw the river he was so disappointed that he refused to stay at Woodstock and took up land farther east in the vicinity of Eastwood.

More will be told of these people when we deal with the homes of Woodstock.

As the province was settled new districts were formed. Oxford became part of the London District which included the counties of Brant, Norfolk, Oxford, Elgin and Middlesex. The district capital was Vittoria until the court house was destroyed by fire in 1825. The seat of government was then moved to London.

In 1837 the District of Brock was formed and eventually Oxford County. In order to become a district it was necessary to have a court house and a gaol. On April 24, 1837 a public meeting was held to consider the erection of the necessary buildings. A building committee was appointed with authority to raise a loan of $12,000. On November 11, 1839, the building was pronounced fit for occupancy and on December 23, 1839, a proclamation was issued setting the District of Brock as a separate district and the town of Woodstock as the district town. The first district council met on February 8, 1842.

Colonel Alexander Light, late of the 25th Regiment of Foot, 1848. (From a watercolor painted by his daughter-in-law.)

A WOODSTOCK BEAR STORY
OF SEVENTY YEARS AGO

Note: This story appears exactly as it appeared in the local press in 1904.

About seventy years ago the ground which now forms the Presbyterian cemetery at Woodstock was the center of as fine a piece of hardwood bush as one could wish to see, hard maples being especially plentiful and many a kettle of the finest maple syrup was boiled down from the sap that came from them. I was a new arrival here at that time having come out from the Old Country in the spring of 1834. During the summer of that year, I, upon the advice of Jacob Karn, who was for those days an old settler and whose home was located west of what is now known as the eleventh line, prepared a supply of sap troughs made from basswood logs to be ready for the maple syrup harvest. I had associated with Samuel Clement and Captain O'Brien, the latter's home being a log house situated near the spot where "Ras" Burgess' residence now stands, and upon part of whose land our operations were conducted.

In the spring of 1835 we commenced tapping the trees, our spiles being of cedar. We fixed our camp on land which is now the cemetery. We borrowed kettles, barrels and tubs where we could and were in fair shape for turning out a plentiful supply of either syrup or sugar. To draw sap to the camp we used an yoke of oxen hitched to a homemade sled upon which we set two barrels; one end of each was removed. The work went merrily on and we were just preparing to sugar off. One of us remained in camp at all times attending to the fire and watching the boiling sap. I had been on duty one night and early in the morning had a fine kettle of syrup done to a turn.

I let the fire down and set the kettle to cool, placing it a short distance from the fire with a red painted barrel, which was used for holding sap, but which at this time was useless, the bung being knocked out. I then settled things in camp so that I could have an hour's rest and turning the empty red barrel over crawled into it for shelter.

I dozed away for some time but was made broadly awake by feeling something nozzle at my feet and looking out saw a huge bear prodding his snout about, evidently in an investigating mood. I felt uncomfortable but realized that my best plan was to remain quiet and a dead man could not have been more still than I was while that bear was taking liberties with my footwear. I guess he thought I wasn't of much account for he presently moved off towards the kettle of cooling syrup.

Here was something that interested him and he immediately stuck his nose in the hot stuff. I could see him through the bung hole of the barrel. It surprised him for he jerked his nose out and backed square against the barrel I was in, shoving his tail through the bung hole and almost hitting me in the eye. He waited for a second or two and then made a second attack on the syrup. In the meantime I had time to make up my mind that if the tail came through the bung hole again I would seize it and hang on, thus making the bear a prisoner in a manner never before heard of. I had hardly come to this decision when slap bang he came again against the barrel, the tail being pushed farther through the bung hole than before. I gripped it with both hands and the fun began.

Did you ever hold a bear's tail stuck through a bung hole? Well, if you didn't I don't see how I can describe adequately what followed.

The bear became ruffled; the mishap to his snout disturbed his temper, but this interference with his tail aggravated him to the pitch of anger. He was getting it at both ends and did not propose to stand it. After emitting an angry grunt the next thing I heard was a furious clawing on the red barrel, but this did no good. The barrel was of stout oak staves with four iron hoops at each end and a head two inches thick. It was made and owned by Thos. Dunn, a carpenter, who came to Woodstock in 1834 and settled with his family on a three-acre lot, near the center of which the CPR station now stands.

His log house was situated in a clearing he made almost directly north of the present Roman Catholic Separate School building. We had borrowed the barrel from him and were to return it sound and in good order after syrup making was over, a gallon of syrup and a pancake of maple sugar to accompany it for its use.

The bear continued his grunting and clawing for a minute or two, I holding onto the tail like grim death, and then started for a tree dragging the barrel over the snow with him. He climbed up a few feet but I held on and he found he could not rid himself of his encumbrance by this means. I suppose he then became alarmed as well as angry, for he slid down the tree and started on the run down the cemetery hill in the direction of the CPR station. Here the bear took a southeasterly course, travelling a little south of Sgt. Eagan's loghouse and passing directly opposite Thomas Dunn's place. Here the procession was seen by Peter Dunn, one of the youngsters, who called the rest of the family crying out at the top of his voice, "Father! Mother! Look at the big dog with a can to his tail."

"Bloody Wars! an' that's my barrel", said Mr. Dunn. "Run, Run! James and call Sergeant Eagan."

Sergeant Eagan was a man of parts in the neighbourhood having been a soldier in one of His Majesty King George IV's Regiments and who would know better than he how to use his firearms? This at any rate was the thought which came to Thos Dunn after it was borne on his mind that to save the red painted barrel, the bear must be shot. Besides, Sgt. Eagan was close at hand. Off James ran to do his errand and by this time the bear, the barrel and I were battling with the stumps, and hillocks, and swampy places that were in existence at that time around the spot where John White's store now stands. The hue and cry was general and the chase was on.

On crossing Hatch's farm, which was bounded on the north side by what is now Dundas Street and was outside the Town Plot, the red barrel became wedged between a fallen log and a tree, a little southeast of the site of the present city hall.

All the efforts of the bear failed to move it and I still held on with a grip of iron. Here Sgt. Eagan and the posse came up with us and it was first discovered that I was inside the barrel. Of course they didn't know it was me until after, but they saw there was a man inside the barrel and there was some careful strategy planned by Sgt. Eagan so as to avoid hitting me when he fired his musket which was loaded with ball. He at last took aim and pulled the trigger but as he pulled the trigger the bear pulled the end of the barrel into range and bang it went into splinters, two or three of them stuck into me and pained quite a little.

"Oh, my barrel", shouted Mr. Dunn. "Bloody Wars, but you've finished it now."

With the blowing out of the end I didn't lose my grip but the bear dragged the loosened barrel free and away we went at a maddening pace. I began to fear that after all my efforts the animal would finally get away. I was as determined as ever to stick to the contest to the last and hoped the pursuers would intercept us in time and shoot the pesky brute. The staves began to rattle. We crossed a stony stretch of ground and the bumping was terrific. Presently the barrel struck a sharp stone that showed a foot above the snow and away went several of the staves. Soon another and another went until every stave and hoop was gone except the stave with the bung hole.

The bear was making terrific time and as we swept through the bush on the Vansittart Estate, the rapidity with which the trees went by made my head spin. The stave with the bung hole grew weak with the constant wearing it received by being dragged along the ground and against the trees. At last the honest oak could stand it no longer and with a bang it went all to pieces and I was hurled violently against a tree.

It was all over! The bear let out a grunt of triumph and rattled away out of sight and I never set eyes on him again. As for me I was knocked out completely and when the posse came up, Sgt. Eagan was carrying his musket at the shoulder, while Mr. Dunn had an armful of staves he had picked up on the way. They found me lying against the tree with nothing but the bung hole of the barrel in my grasp to show that such a fierce race had been run. But I've said often and often, that I'll never forget that bear.

EARLY SCHOOLS OF WOODSTOCK

The first school in Woodstock was established in 1817. A small log building was erected at the corner of Dundas and Chapel Streets which contained four windows, a door and a fireplace. There were two rows of desks and benches, one on each side of the room, and at one end stood the teacher's high desk. There were no blackboards, or maps. The ink was made by boiling bark of the soft maple with copperas and it was made frost-proof by adding a little whiskey. A bucket of water from a nearby spring provided the drinking water.

The first master was Dr. Levi Hoyt Perry. He was born in Litchfield, Conn., and was educated for the Presbyterian ministry. Dr. Perry obtained his degree in medicine at Sturbridge, Mass. He married Esther Burtch, a daughter of Zachias Burtch, and settled in Woodstock. He conducted classes during the winter months, this being the only time of the year when students were available. Another master was Wm. H. Langdon, who was also the elder who acted as minister of the Baptist congregation until an ordained minister was obtained in 1854. He was president of Woodstock's Subscription Library which was one of the first such libraries in Upper Canada, County Superintendent of Schools and County Clerk during his lifetime.

School books were scarce and were handed down from father to son. Canada had not established an educational system and the text books were of English or American publication.

The early speller also acted as a primer. It began with the alphabet in the different forms of type, followed by simple three-letter words followed by more difficult words, then simple phrases and finally sentences and a form of catechism.

The English reader known as "Murray's English Reader", was designed to improve the highest class of learners in reading, to establish a taste for just and accurate composition and to promote the interests of piety and virtue. It was a very serious book.

Grammar was taught from two text books, "Lennie's English Grammar" and "Murray's Grammar". Walkingame's Arithmetic covered its subject thoroughly.

Woodstock's second school was built in 1839 by subscription and was located on Dundas St. east of Bay. This school was known as "Goodwin's School" after its teacher, Christopher Goodwin. The building also served as the village hall and meeting house for all denominations lacking a place of worship. It was later moved to Bay St., became a private dwelling and is still standing today.

The first school trustees were Henry Bishop, R. R. Hunter, John Greig and Robert Lynn.

An Act of Parliament passed in 1841 provided for the appointment of a school superintendent, but two years later this was abolished and county councils appointed local superintendents as needed.

LATER SCHOOLS

The groundwork for Grammar Schools (secondary schools) and for universities was laid by Sir John Graves Simcoe in 1796, but he was recalled to England before he was able to put it into practice. In 1798 the Imperial Government recommended that four grammar schools be established at Cornwall, Kingston, Newark and Sandwich, but no action was taken. In 1807, 500 pounds was voted for support of eight grammar schools but none were established. In 1839, 250,000 acres of land were set aside for their endowment. The first Grammar School established in Western Ontario was at Woodstock in 1843.

The first three years of the grammar school was in conjunction with the common school with John Somerville, the principal, acting as the teacher. The trustees then refused to allow grammar school subjects to be taught here any longer and a building was obtained at the corner of Dundas and Wellington Sts. This building was later known as the Central Hotel. The master of the school was to receive one hundred pounds per year, and such fees as he could collect. For the one hundred pounds he was obliged to teach ten students free of charge. Mr. Somerville remained until 1846 when he resigned and was replaced by Geo. Strauchon, B.A., who was appointed by the Governor-General. Prior to his coming to Woodstock he had been a teacher at Queen's College in Kingston.

Left — *Advertisements clipped from "Woodstock Herald" issues of 1847. Right* — *Mrs. Martha Dancer, who came to Woodstock as Martha Barton, governess to the Rev. Bettridge's children and who later opened a private school of her own in the Town.*

The school remained at this site for five years, with the principal paying the rent and providing the desks, etc., for the students. The attendance was approximately 25 students, with Latin, Greek, Mathematics and English the main subjects. Only students of exceptional talent attended.

The brick grammar school was erected on the corner of Graham and Hunter St. in 1851 and Principal Strauchon remained as headmaster. He remained for thirty years and earned the title of "The father of Secondary Education in Woodstock". His first assistant was Wm. Oliver who later became headmaster at Brantford. By 1881 the staff had increased to four.

The grammar school became overcrowded and in 1881 it was necessary to build a larger school. This was erected on Riddell and is now known as the Woodstock Collegiate and Vocational Institute. Three years later Mr. Strauchon stepped down as principal but remained on the staff for five years as classical master specializing in Latin. He was succeeded by D. H. Hunter as principal (1884).

and discipline were taught and students (Modelites) visited the different public schools to observe the technique of trained teachers. These model schools operated during the fall term and the graduates received a third class teacher's certificate. They were abolished in 1907 and Normal Schools took their place.

Woodstock's first common school was erected on Graham St. at a cost of approximately $900.00. It was staffed by four teachers, Christopher Goodwin, Henry Izzard, Mrs. Walkinshaw, and Mrs. Martha Snarey. The school superintendent was Rev. Wm. Ball and the tuition fee was 2s 6d per quarter.

Left — Woodstock Grammar School (left) and the old Methodist Church in 1865. Right — The Collegiate Institute and Principal I. M. Levan, in 1901.

In 1886 the status of the school was raised to that of a High School. Mr. Hunter remained until his death in 1898. He was succeeded by I. M. Levan. On the staff at that time was A. D. Griffin, C. A. Kerr, E. C. Srigley, J. M. Cole, C. F. Erret and Miss Carrie Fair.

As the town grew so did the school, and from time to time new rooms and classes were added. Manual training, household science and a commercial department were among the major additions.

A common school teacher could obtain his or her license to teach originally by having an education and being a specialist in penmanship. Later this was changed and it was necessary for those wishing to enter the teaching profession to be examined by a board of county examiners, the succccessful applicants being granted a teaching certificate. In 1877 Model Schools were established. School management

The public school system of the province of Ontario was introduced in 1850. Dr. Edgar Ryerson was appointed to lead this department and was assisted by Rev. John Strachan, a cousin of George Strachan of the Grammar School.

Two brick schools were erected to relieve the pressure on the common school. One was in the east end and the other in the west end. Today the sites are occupied by Princess and Victoria Schools. The cost of these schools was about $7,000 each and they were built for service and not for looks. Heat was supplied by huge box stoves and on cold days it was necessary for the students to continually change places in order that at least once during the day they would be warm. The water pail was replaced by a green wooden pump with several tin cups chained to it. The blackboards occupied at least one wall and very modern desks were installed after many heated debates by the trustees.

Mr. Goodwin was appointed principal of the East End school and Miss McDonald, his assistant. Henry Izzard was principal of the West End school, with Mr. Hughes and Miss L. Piper his assistants. The trustees were Col. G. W. Whitehead, John Douglas, Rev. Wm. Langdon, Alex Green, F. B. Scofield and Andrew Smith.

These were not the only schools in the town. There were still residents who preferred to have their children go to private schools, especially girls, where they could learn to become ladies. The first of the private schools was opened in 1851 and was located on Chapel St., with Mrs. Henry Revell in charge. Her husband, Rev. Henry Revell, had been the first resident Anglican clergyman in Ingersoll and due to ill health had resigned and come to Woodstock. Mrs. Revell conducted the school until 1861 when her daughter, Mrs. Minty, took charge and the school was moved to Graham St. Mrs. Revell joined the staff of the Literary Institute and gave instruction in music.

Another school was opened in September, 1856, with Mrs. Walkinshaw in charge. It was located at 375 Simcoe St., had an enrollment of four but the attendance increased and spacious quarters were sought. The school operated by Mrs. Minty was a school for a select group of young ladies. Former students tell of the perfect deportment and dignified manner of Mrs. Minty who successfully carried on her school until 1881. The governess at this school was Miss Bretts, a very timid lady. It was said that she never appeared in public unless she had at least three veils over her face to protect her complexion.

Another early teacher who later conducted her own school, was Mrs. Martha Snarey. She was the governess for the Bettridge children when she came to Canada in 1834 and was one of the eleven present at the first service conducted in Old St. Paul's Church. She conducted a private school at her home on Norwich Ave. and admitted both boys and girls. After the death of Mr. Snarey, she married a Mr. Dancer and operated a private school on Canterbury St. just off Riddell.

Other private schools included one conducted by a Miss Nesbitt at Dundas Cottage; another operated by Miss Cummings on Market St., advertised that English, French, Italian, German and Latin were taught, as was the piano, harp and organ. Prof. VanHoxar's School for Boys was a popular school. Misses Mary and Isabel Short also had a school.

Compulsory attendance at school for at least four months became law in the passing of the School Act of 1871. It was not until 1889 that a truant officer was hired to enforce the act. Wm. Baldwin received this appointment with a salary of $40.00 per year.

In 1878 the trustees of Woodstock's Public Schools purchased from the Vestry of Old St. Paul's a certain parcel of land known as "The Court House Square". This was part of the Clergy Reserve and one of the last grants made. The first principal was J. E. Dennis. One of the outstanding principals was J. W. Garvin. He resigned as principal in 1893 to become inspector at Peterborough. In 1897 he originated a new educational policy for the Conservative Government of Ontario. One of the recommendations called for the abolition of the Model Schools and the adoption of the Normal School method of training teachers with more normal schools being opened throughout the province.

THE OXFORD RIFLES

Few people of Woodstock and Oxford County are aware that the Oxford Rifles, the County Militia Regiment, is one of the senior and most distinguished regiments of the Militia of Canada. The former title of the 22nd Regiment indicates that it was the twenty-second militia regiment to be organized in the Dominion, another fact which is not generally known. For more than a century, Oxford County has been an active militia centre, for while the 22nd Regiment, the Oxford Rifles, was organized in the year 1863, the Oxford Militia was organized in 1798.

The history of the militia in Oxford County commences with the birth of the county by the act of 1798 altering the territorial divisions of Upper Canada. The village of Burford, now in Brant County, was the home of a company of the First York Militia and this company formed the nucleus of four companies designated the First Regiment, Oxford Militia, which Col. William Claus was authorized to raise on his appointment as lieutenant of the county. The four companies were known as the Burford, Blenheim, 1st and 2nd Oxford Companies. Capt. Thomas Ingersoll, Sr., commanded the 2nd Oxford Company.

In the War of 1812, the Oxford Militia was called out for active service, taking part in the capture of Fort Detroit, the engagement at Fort Erie and Lundy's Lane and the fight at Malcolm's Mills against a party of American raiders.

A point of interest in connection with the war was that Thomas Horner, the first settler in Oxford County and afterwards M.P. for the riding, offered to organize the Oxford Militia and take them to the war, but as he had resided in the United States, the authorities doubted his loyalty and refused to give him permission. The refusal did not stem Thomas Horner's feelings of patriotism and he organized a body of Indians, which he led to the war.

Provision was made in 1838 for the organization of five separate corps in the County of Oxford, one at Burford, one within the limits of Blenheim, Blandford and Woodstock, one in the Township of Zorra, one in the Townships of Burford and Oakland, and the other within the limits of Nissouri, East, West and North Oxford.

By act of 1851, Brant County was formed and the five units split up in a reorganization according to the new county boundaries. The Oxford Militia remained active as a county organization until its organization as the 22nd Regiment in 1863. The 22nd Regiment continued until the outbreak of war in 1914, having become a city corps in 1907. During the war, Oxford County sent her men overseas in the 71st Battalion and the 168th Battalion, "Oxford's Own", as well as in other overseas units, and drafts for the 1st, 18th and 36th Battalions C.E.F. After the war the militia unit was reorganized and renamed by the single title of "Oxford Rifles".

An interesting fact in connection with the organization of the Oxford Rifles is that among the county companies which formed the regiment originally was a Highland Volunteer Militia Rifle Company which was organized at Embro in the previous year.

During the history of the Oxford Rifles prior to the Great War, three calls were made on it for service. The first occasion was in December 1864, when No. 1 Company (Woodstock), and No. 3 Company (Beachville) of the Oxford Rifles, formed Nos. 1 and 2 Companies of the Eastern Battalion of the three battalions drawn from the militia regiments for frontier service at Laprairie, Quebec, at the time when fears were felt for Fenians crossing from the United States. Major Hugh Richardson commanded the Woodstock Company and Capt. Greig, the Beachville unit, while the officer in command of the Eastern Battalion, composed of companies from several regiments, was also chosen from Woodstock in Lt. Col. John B. Taylor, O.C. the Oxford Rifles.

The second call on the regiment was made in November, 1865, when a company with Capt. H. B. Beard, Lieut. John Matheson and Ensign James Coad as its officers was sent to Sarnia for similar frontier service. Lt. Col. J. B. Taylor of the Rifles was again placed in command of the battalion at this border point.

On facing page — The 22nd Regiment at the head of Perry St. (looking south) 1866.

While the company was at Sarnia, Lt. Col. J. B. Taylor was attached to Major General Napier's staff as Deputy Assistant Adjutant General for Volunteer Corps, placed on service in the Western districts. Upon Lt. Col. Taylor's promotion, Major Hugh Richardson, also of the Oxford Rifles, was placed in command of the battalion at Sarnia and also made Lt. Col. in command of the local regiment.

At the time of the Fenian Raid in March, 1866, the companies of Woodstock, Thamesford, Ingersoll, Embro, North Oxford, Drumbo, Princeton and Paris were called out for active service but were not however taken into action.

On the first of June, 1866, the Ingersoll and Drumbo infantry companies were ordered out together with the remaining companies of the Oxford Rifles. It is said that when notice was received in Woodstock, the company paraded in full marching order three-quarters of an hour after the first bugle call.

On June 8, Capt. McCleneghan's company was authorized as the Woodstock Infantry Company and was ordered to London for actual service. In the meantime, the companies ordered out on the first of June had been sent to the frontier where they arrived just too late to take part in the fight at Ridgeway. They detrained at Port Colborne, marched to Fort Erie, taking prisoner 65 Fenians on the way there. They remained two days at Fort Erie and returned to London where they were retained on duty for nearly two weeks. Capt. McCleneghan's company was sent to Sandwich.

In 1868 there occurred the only case in the County of Oxford in which the militia was called out in aid of the civil power. William Grey was mayor of Woodstock and twenty N.C.O.'s and men under Capt. (afterwards Lt. Col.) Beard, were required to disperse a crowd which had collected and threatened two "whiskey detectives".

Capt. McCleneghan was in 1871 one of the members of the Canadian team that took part in the rifle matches at Wimbledon Common. Lt. Col. Skinner of North Oxford was also instrumental in organizing the team and commanded it on the trip to England.

The following is the order by which the Oxford Rifles came into being dated August 14, 1863: "The six Volunteer Militia Rifle Companies under the command of the following officers are hereby formed into a battalion under the provisions of Section 26 of the Consolidated Militia Law and will be styled 'The Twenty-Second Battalion Volunteer Militia Rifles Canada' or 'The Oxford Rifles'. The headquarters will be at Woodstock and the companies will be numbered as follows, viz:

"Capt. Hugh Richardson, No. 1 Company, Woodstock; Capt. Isaac Wallace, No. 2 Company (Highland), Embro; Capt. Geo. Greig, No. 3 Company, Beachville; Capt. Louis B. Cole, No. 4 Company, Wolverton; Capt. John Henderson, No. 5 Company, North Oxford; Capt. Cowan, No. 6 Company, Princeton.

"To be Lt. Col. of this battalion, Lt. Col. W. S. Light, Brigade Major of the Eighth Mil. Dis."

Proceeding through the records, it is interesting to note that in the London Division in 1864, the 1st Company of the Oxford Rifles won the 2nd, 3rd and 4th prizes for efficiency.

Lt. Col. Light's death followed very closely on the issuing of the above order and the reorganization of the regiment was hardly commenced until Major John B. Taylor was in May 1864 promoted to the command. The funeral of Lt.-Col. Light was held with military honors and was one of the most impressive that Woodstock has seen. A cortege of about two miles in length followed the bier.

At the end of 1865 a militia list gives the following strength of the Oxford Rifles: John B. Taylor, Lt.-Col. in command with Hugh Richardson as Major, and James White as adjutant.

No. 1 Coy., Woodstock, under Capt. Henry Beard with Stephen A. Scott, M.D., as surgeon; No. 2 Coy., (Highland), Embro, under Capt. George Duncan with L. H. Swan, M.D., as surgeon; No. 3 Coy., North Oxford, under Capt. George Greig; No. 5 Coy., North Oxford, under Capt. John Henderson with Henry Brown as Ensign; No. 6 Coy., Princeton, under Capt. Thomas Cowan.

It will be noticed that No. 4 Coy. at Wolverton is not mentioned. The company although authorized was not organized. There were also three independent companies at the time, namely: Thamesford Infantry Coy., under Capt. Thomas Dawes; Ingersoll Infantry Coy., under Capt. G. Wonham, and Drumbo Infantry Coy., under Capt. Wesley Howell.

The 22nd Regimental Band in 1870. Sgt. Bandsman Deverell appears fourth from the left in the front row while Bandmaster Marchant is seventh from the left in the back row. The bass drummer is W. H. "Oklahoma Bill" Murray.

The 4th Company of the regiment at Wolverton was officially disbanded in 1866 and was replaced by a company at Norwich under the temporary captaincy of John W. Nesbitt. In the same year, the strength of the regiment grew to 10 companies with the addition of infantry companies at Ingersoll, East Oxford, Lakeside and Mount Elgin, and one other at Woodstock. In 1869 the force was re-enrolled in nine companies at Woodstock, Embro, Princeton, Ingersoll, Norwich, East Oxford and Lakeside.

In the records from 1870 onwards, the names of well-known Woodstock citizens made constant appearances. Ensign M. M. Nesbitt was in 1871 appointed to be lieutenant, and a year later was appointed as captain. The names of others come to note as the pages of the records are turned over. D. M. Perry was appointed Ensign in 1870.

Lt.-Col. Hugh Richardson was permitted in 1875 to retire from the command of the regiment, becoming stipendiary magistrate in the Northwest Territories, and Major Thomas Cowan became the commanding officer, with Major H. B. Beard second in command. In the orders of 1880, the appointment of Alfred Servos Ball, later police magistrate, as lieutenant is made. The following year, another prominent barrister, James Carruthers Hegler, was appointed lieutenant of No. 4 Company at Ingersoll. In this year D. R. Ross became 2nd Lieut. in the Embro Company, which he later commanded. His sons, J. G. Ross and J. M. Ross, were also officers at a later date.

In the orders of 1882, the authorization of the regiment's badge is made in these terms: "This Battalion is authorized to use the following badge and motto:— A Maltese cross, having at each of its angles a British lion and in the centre, the numerals 22 encircled by the additional designation of the Battalion, 'The Oxford Rifles', the whole encircled by a wreath of maple leaves, the whole surmounted by an Imperial crown with the motto 'Pro Aris et Focis' on the wreath at the base of the badge."

Lt.-Col. Cowan retired in 1885 and Lt.-Col. James Munro of Embro took command. Col. Munro was chosen as one of the officers of the Canadian contingent at Queen Victoria's Diamond Jubilee.

Capt. A. R. McCleneghan of the Strathallan Company was appointed paymaster in 1885 and James Sutherland, later minister of public works, was appointed to the rank of captain. Capt. Sutherland was the next year made quartermaster and Lieut. A. S. Ball was promoted to the rank of captain. Later Capt. Sutherland was given the honorary rank of major in the active militia, as a special case. Many other prominent men of the county were also officers of the regiment.

On facing page — Part of the 22nd Regiment (Oxford Rifles) as they relaxed during training in the fall of 1898. Mr. A. S. Ball (back row with beard and civilian cap), D. M. Sutherland (to the left of Mr. Ball) and other officers of the Regiment will be recognized by many. This page, left — Two well-known and respected members of the 22nd Regimental Band as they appeared about 1870. On the left is Bandmaster Marchant and on the right, Sgt. Bandsman (later Bandmaster) Deverell.

Above — Three Woodstock officers at Camp Windsor, June 24th, 1872. From the left they are Ensign Coad, Capt. Beard and Lt. Perry.

The orders of 1895 contain the appointment of Frederick O. Burgess to be second lieutenant. Mr. Burgess was later Lieut.-Col. of the regiment and the collector of customs for this district. Capt. A. S. Ball was in 1896 appointed quartermaster, which rank he held until his retirement and a year later was given the honorary rank of major.

Two other appointments in 1896 are of note, namely those of John Munro Ross and William Frederick Mackay, both to be second lieutenants. The former became Brigadier General Ross and the latter is a brother of Lt.-Col. C. Mackenzie Mackay, O.C. the Oxford Rifles in 1927. Lt.-Col. J. C. Hegler succeeded Col. Munro as O.C. in 1898. Dr. A. T. Rice and Dr. Hugh Mackay were well known surgeon officers at that time.

Dr. J. M. Rogers of Ingersoll was in 1898 appointed surgeon lieutenant, and the Rev. J. C. Farthing, later Bishop of Montreal, was made honorary chaplain, while G. R. Pattullo Jr. became second lieutenant. The same year the appointment is noted of D. M. Sutherland to be lieutenant; J. G. Dunlop was in 1900 appointed second lieutenant.

In 1906 the regiment was reorganized, the officers being permitted to retire, and the changes to a city corps effected.

A notable fact was that all the retiring staff officers were in possession of the long service medal.

R.Q.M.S. James Brown, who with Major W. L. Kerr and Corporal J. Cross, the only member of the regiment who was a member at the reorganization in 1907, also had some interesting original documents connected with the history of the Oxford Rifles. These old records included the Regiment's first service roll as well as the orderly book with the first entry signed by A. W. Francis, orderly sergeant, and the orderly book of the Ingersoll Company which contained the orders given to the company at the time the militia went to Sarnia. The first

On facing page — The ceremony on the Court House lawn at the dedication (1902) of the statue of Colour Sgt. George W. Leonard, 22nd Regiment (The Oxford Rifles) who died of wounds the previous year at Zand River, South Africa. The statue, a bronze bust of the Sgt., was sculptured in 1901 by F. A. T. Dunbar. The entire Regiment attended this dedication. This page — A parade of the Regiment in front of the City Hall at the turn of the century. Part of the City of Woodstock Band can be seen in the foreground.

of these entries was the copy of an order from Major Hugh Richardson at Woodstock to Capt. Wonham, "Turn out men in two hours at any sacrifice and report by telegraph at one p.m."

Other interesting documents included the service roll of No. 7 Coy., in 1885, the Battalion order book, commencing 1879, a crime sheet of 1895, the correspondence files of 1863 and the service roll of 1887. R.Q.M.S. Brown also had the commission of Hedley Vicars Knight as major.

The new officer commanding the 22nd in 1907 was Lt. Col. John White with Major (subsequently Lt. Col.) W. T. McMullen as second in command. J. M. Ross (brigadier general) was adjutant. Capt. Fred Millman commanded A. Company, Capt. (subsequently Lt. Col.) F. O. Burgess, B. Company, Capt. T. L. Hay, C. Company, and Capt. W. J. Taylor, D. Company. The subalterns of the new city corps were Lieutenants Wallace Elmslie and Charles Shedden, in A. Company, W. L. Kerr and A. E. Woodroofe in B. Company, J. G. Dunlop in C. Company, and R. F. Parkinson, afterwards in command of the 38th Overseas Regiment and later O.C. the Governor General's Foot Guards, and G. S. Pepper in D. Company. Capt. F. Crossley was quartermaster, Capt. Malcolm Douglas, paymaster, Lieut. A. B. Welford, medical officer, and the Rev. R. B. Cochrane, chaplain.

Lt. Col. White continued in command of the unit until 1912 when Major McMullen became Lt. Col. in command.

From the reorganization of the regiment until the outbreak of the Great War, the Oxford Rifles was one of the most popular institutions in the city of Woodstock, the four companies being constantly at full strength.

The present splendid Armory was built at the time of reorganization and with its large gymnasium floor, bowling alley and sporting facilities, it became the centre of some of the best sport organizations in the city. All the year round various competitions were in progress for trophies presented by officers and citizens interested in the local militia unit. Each company and special unit had teams competing in the contests for trophies in basketball, bowling and shooting within the regiment, while the regiment had very good teams in the city sporting contests as well.

In addition to showing great keenness in sports the members of the regiment were no less keen in their military training. Large turnouts were present at the regular parades and a very fine esprit de corps present throughout the organization.

The training during the pre-war years included a number of interesting trips each year. These events during that time included camps at Goderich and London. One year the Regiment took part in manoeuvres in the Dundas district, which included a sham fight between Militia units of Military District Numbers 1 and 2. There was also a sham fight held locally by the regiment at Burgess Flats. One year the regiment took part in a celebration at Hamilton and another summer, the unit took part in a July 1 celebration at Port Dover, spending the weekend under canvas.

On August 4, 1914, Great Britain declared war on Germany and in Woodstock Lt. Col. McMullen issued a call to officers, N.C.O.'s and other ranks of the Regiment to report for duty. An instantaneous response was made to the call and on the evening of August 5 the Oxford Rifles paraded the streets of Woodstock.

On August 22, seventy men, headed by Lieut. Cecil James (killed in action at Festubert) left Woodstock to join the first Canadian contingent at Valcartier camp. These men formed two platoons or half of "A" Company of the First Battalion under the command of Major, now Lt. Col. D. M. Sutherland.

The Oxford County men of the 1st Battalion were among the first soldiers of the 1st Canadian Division to go into the trenches in France and distinguished themselves at the battle of Langemarck, where Lieut. James and his fellow Oxonians were in the first platoons to advance under the fire of the German infantry and were the first to undergo the experience of having poison gas used as a weapon against them.

In September, 1914, 150 men left Woodstock and were attached to "D" Company of the 18th Battalion.

Another body of men led by Lieut. Guy Sawtell was organized a little later by Lt. Col. McMullen and this draft became part of the 34th Battalion at London, Ont. The 34th Battalion went overseas with the second contingent.

Returning to Canada after being wounded in service with the 1st Battalion, Major D. M. Sutherland was given the rank of Lt. Col. and authorized to raise the 71st Battalion from the counties of Oxford, Perth, Waterloo, Wellington, Huron and Bruce. Oxford County furnished one company and the headquarters. Five hundred and thirty-eight men exclusive of officers were recruited in Oxford County under the general order which was dated August 28, 1915. As fast as recruits were sworn in they were sent in drafts to London where they were outfitted and their training commenced.

In November 1915, the regiment went into winter quarters in Woodstock, Chatham, Stratford, and Guelph, where they were accommodated in the Armories. The local Armory on Graham Street was the scene of great activity during the winter of 1915-16.

On April 1, 1916, the regiment sailed from Halifax on the S.S. Olympic. Arriving at Liverpool, the battalion was moved to Bramshott camp and then to Oxney Camp at Borden, Hants. The regiment was then broken up and furnished drafts to line battalions in Canadian divisions.

The men who left Woodstock in the 71st Battalion were engaged on the Western Front in all actions on the Canadian portion of the front from June 1, 1916, to the close of the war. Within ten months from the authorization of the 71st Battalion, the men composing it were in action.

Two officers of the 71st Battalion have since the war commanded the Oxford Rifles. They were then Major F. O. Burgess and Capt. C. Mackenzie Mackay.

Top — Several members of the Regiment pose on the cannon (later placed on the Court House lawn) in Victoria Park in 1900. This photo was printed from the original glass negative. Bottom — The "new" Armoury in 1906. This photo was taken on Jan. 30th of that year and shows oldtimers enjoying lawn bowling in the middle of winter.

On December 21st, 1915, authority was given Lt. Col. McMullen to raise the 168th Battalion, which became known as "Oxford's Own". Fresh numbers of the county's manhood responded to the new call and on June 1st, 1916, the battalion went into camp at London, having reached the full strength of nine hundred and forty-three officers and other ranks.

After brief training at Camp Francis in London, the battalion was sent to Camp Borden on July 9th. Four months were spent at Borden in intensive training and on October 27th, seven hundred and thirteen men (some of the originals having been transferred to other units) left for Halifax and from there to Liverpool.

On arrival in England, the battalion was sent to West Sandling Camp where the men were taken on strength of the 12th and 39th Reserve Battalions and training was completed.

Although the 168th had ceased to exist in name, the men from Oxford fought from January 1st, 1917, to November 11th, 1918. Of the seven hundred and thirteen men who sailed from Canada, one hundred and fifty-eight did not return, a loss of twenty-two percent of the strength. Two hundred and fifty-six were wounded, making total casualties of four hundred and fourteen or fifty-eight percent.

Men of this unit, reinforcing service battalions in France, took part in all operations of the Canadian Corps subsequent to January 1st, 1917. Among the principal actions in which men from Oxford took part were Vimy Ridge, Hill 70, Passchendaele, Amiens, the Second Battle of Arras, Cambrai, Valenciennes and Mons.

At the close of the war in 1919, Lt. Col. Burgess took over the command of the 22nd Regiment and continued in this capacity until 1922, when Lt. Col. C. Mackenzie Mackay succeeded him. Lt. Col. Mackay, who had served in the old county corps, had rejoined the city corps in 1909 as lieutenant and served overseas with the 71st Battalion.

In 1920 a change was made in the nomenclature of the Oxford Rifles in common with other militia units in the Dominion, in the case of the local regiment, the title "22nd Regiment" being dropped. The reason for the change is given as follows:

In 1919 following the close of the war, a board of officers under the presidency of Sir William Otter, assembled for the purpose of considering the reorganization of the Militia of Canada and a change in the nomenclature of units in order that former units of the Active Militia of Canada, upon reorganization, would perpetuate the traditions of the C.E.F. units created during the period of the War.

This board visited every district in Canada taking evidence from all officers commanding, with the result that the consensus of opinion of all those interested in militia matters was that the territorial system of nomenclature should be adopted for infantry regiments, the battalions of which should be numbered from one up, consecutively, and that the C.E.F. unit would be perpetuated by inserting in brackets after the Regimental name, the C.E.F. Battalion to be so perpetuated.

In the case of the Woodstock Regiment, the recommendations made by the committee were as follows:

"The Oxford Rifles; 1st Bn. (71st Bn., C.E.F.);
Reserve Battalion, 2nd Bn. (168th Bn., C.E.F.)."

After the war the interest of citizens in the Oxford Rifles seemed to return but slowly although each training season has showed improvement. The 1925 fall training season proved a gratifying success with great interest and enthusiasm being shown by a large number of new members. The signal section proved very popular and did excellent work.

In connection with the militia of Oxford County, it is necessary to make mention of Grey's Horse, a cavalry regiment that was organized in the county with Woodstock as its headquarters, and had a number of prominent men of the county in its staff of officers. After the war, however, the headquarters of the regiment was transferred from Woodstock to Wingham, Ontario, and there is practically no longer any local connection beyond its origin and the fact that Lt. Col. D. M. Sutherland is Honorary Colonel of the Regiment.

Grey's Horse was organized in 1908 by Lt. Col. W. M. Davis, a former resident of Woodstock, at that time resident in Kitchener. The organization meeting was held in Woodstock and Woodstock became the headquarters of the regiment.

In the first organization there were two squadrons in Oxford County, one at Ingersoll and one at Woodstock. "A" Squadron at Woodstock was under the command of J. M. Ross with D. M. Sutherland as second in command. "B" Squadron at Ingersoll was under the command of T. R. Mayberry. Among the other officers were James Pullin and James Bastedo of Sweaburg.

Two years after the organization, Lt. Col. T. R. Mayberry succeeded to the command and continued in command until after the war when the regiment was reorganized with headquarters at Wingham.

Grey's Horse was a very active unit prior to the war. Each year the regiment went to camp, taking a large number of men from all parts of the county on the trip.

When war broke out in August, 1914, Grey's Horse immediately commenced to mobilize in Ingersoll as the Oxford Rifles were assembling in Woodstock. At the same time as Lieut. James left Woodstock with his seventy men, Major D. M. Sutherland left Ingersoll for Valcartier with the Grey's Horse contingent of fifty men. At Valcartier, both the men of the Oxford Rifles and Grey's Horse were drafted into "A" Company of the First Battalion.

After the war, Grey's Horse transferred its headquarters to Wingham and its active connection with Oxford County ceased. Lt. Col. Moss succeeded Col. Mayberry as the O.C.

On second previous page — In 1949, the summer training of the Oxford Rifles included all types of infantry warfare and in this photo, taking a lesson in the maintenance of a Bren Gun Carrier are (left to right) Lt. Jim Bassett, Cpl. J. A. Turner and Lt. Harold Major.

On facing page — Although Woodstock is an inland City, many of her sons served in services other than with the local Regiment. Here we see H.M.C.S. Woodstock, a pitching, rolling, cramped but tough little fighting Corvette, named after the City and on whom many local men served during World War II.

The following poem was written by an unknown Woodstonian and appeared in the local press shortly after the death of a renowned Town Character, Elijah Brown.

ODE TO ELIJAH BROWN

Old Elijah Brown is dead and gone,
We miss him every day,
They took him to the Potter's field
And covered him with clay.

No fancy hearse conveyed him there,
No flowers were on his bier,
No funeral cortege draped in crepe,
No one to shed a tear.

No eulogies on him were said,
Who filled a pauper's grave,
A board to mark the spot is all
Of "Nigger Brown", the slave.

A chequered life Elijah lived,
A century or more,
Though black his face, his heart was white
And honest, to the core.

Rest there in peace my coloured friend
Till Gabriel blows his horn,
You'll rise and walk the golden streets,
Though here, you suffered scorn.

WOODSTOCK, THE TOWN

Woodstock's police force during 1890's consisted of Constables Prompt and Vigorous during the daylight hours and Marsh and Seeker during the hours of darkness.

The political life of the community in this book is divided into two parts; one, the town and the other, the city. The word "political" does not necessarily mean who the mayor and councillors were but is used as a figure of speech to cover some of the aspects of life that were either directly or indirectly controlled by the town fathers.

Prior to January 1, 1851, Woodstock was referred to as "The Town of Woodstock", chiefly because of the term "Town Plot" which had been used by Sir John Graves Simcoe when he designated the spot as a site for a future townsite. An unofficial census taken in 1845 by George Menzies, editor of the weekly newspaper, gave the population of the community as slightly over 1,000 souls.

In 1851, an official census was taken by Thos. Shenstone, the county clerk, who listed the population as 2,112 souls, 240 frame houses and 47 brick houses. There were six houses in the course of construction and eight vacant. This census was taken on orders from the Legislative Assembly which had proclaimed the community a town as of January 1, 1851. The Earl of Elgin had signed the official decree.

The first election for town council was held January 6 and 7, 1851. Ordinarily only one day would have been necessary for the vote, but

Warwick Bookbinders, Parker and Hood Clothing and Dr. Alfred Scott, Druggist. The lamp is in front of the Prince of Wales Saloon, then we see Peddie Dry Goods, Rippon Dry Goods, Grinton Dry Goods, Richmond Furs, Pearson's Flour and Feed and on the Riddell St. corner, Parr's Grocery. These buildings are also quite recognizable today.

The photo above, left, did not win world-wide fame but depicts much more sentiment than many that did. It was taken about a mile south of Woodstock in 1865 and shows two well-known characters in the history of this city. "Shanty" McGee, a pugilist of local repute, is the fiddler, two neighbouring farmers listen, and the colored gentleman, buried in thought, is "Gil" Sanders, who later became a local barber. When this picture was taken, "Gil" had just arrived here, having made his escape from slavery in the South. He was crossing the fields when the music, perhaps a southern melody, arrested his attention. In this deeply reminiscent frame of mind, photographer James Nicholson, who happened to be passing the barn at that moment, caught him. Upper right shows "Gil" a few years later.

On facing page — Top — This is the west side of Vansittart Ave. looking north in 1865. Behind the trees is a dwelling built by Thos. Phelan. The Vulcan Foundry and Wm. Wilson's dwelling and wagon shop, the oldest in Woodstock, are next. The lower photo also shows Vansittart Ave. (1865) but is the east side looking north. Among the businesses in this block were the Garner and Rose Carriage Works, a wagon shop, bowling alley and carpenter shop. In the upper left of the photo is the home now owned by Mr. H. R. Henderson, a beautiful example of early Victorian architecture.

On the two preceding pages — Left page — You are looking at the north side of Dundas St. from Light St. west, in 1865. From right to left, the businesses at that time were Dingwell's Jewellery, Beard and Nellis Barristers, Braidwood's Dry Goods (in the old Manchester House), Bickel's Meat Market, Oliver and Schell's General Store, a barber shop, Donaldson's Meat Market (a well-known Zorra farmer), Gunn's Grocery, Harwood's Confectionery, a saloon formerly owned by Jos. Dorman, a druggist, a bookseller, a tavern, a feed store and a boot shop. At Vansittart Ave. can be seen the North American Hotel. A number of these buildings are still standing and can be recognized today. Right page — This is also the north side of Dundas St. in 1865 looking east to Riddell St. On the left is the John White Co. under construction, followed by Dease and Chambers,

a second day was allowed due to the conditions of the roads. This reason for the action is dubious as it was more than likely due to the fact that as a result of the closeness of the vote, a second day was required to try and get enough voters out to make a decision possible. When the votes were finally tabulated, the results were: Wm. Wilson, 99 votes, Valentine Hall 98, Hugh Richardson 94, Alex Green 92, and Andrew Smith 90. The following day the council selected Hugh Richardson to act as reeve. Thos. Kintrea was appointed the town clerk and Thos. Scott as town treasurer.

The town bylaw #1 was a routine act covering the governing of the town. Bylaw #2 was a revenue bylaw licensing the keepers of inns, beer and ale houses. Bylaw #5 controlled the movements of horses and cattle within the town limits if diseased. This could be considered the first bylaw controlling the cutting of weeds and disposal of garbage, as horses and cattle were ideal for this purpose. Bylaw #9 set the rate of pay for the town officers.

The new council was anxious to do good for the town and decided that a drain down the hill into Cedar Creek was necessary and proceded to have the job done. The ratepayers set up a storm of protest which caused the defeat of the council after only one year in office.

This protest divided the town into two camps, the east versus the west. The east proved to be the stronger of the two and won the election the following year. It appears that the old council poured all their funds down the drain as it became necessary for the new council to issue a debenture for 23 pounds 5 shillings to be retired in five years (at the present rate of $3.04 per pound, it would amount to $70.68).

Warner Barnard was appointed town constable to enforce law and order and to supervise the conduct in the town's 13 grog shops, 7 hotels and 9 taverns. On these premises drinks could be consumed by the glass.

Livery stables, blacksmith shops and grocery stores had permits to sell to the farm trade in bulk, the price being one shilling per gallon. Eating houses usually supplied a jolt to "whet your appetite" before meals. Later, Bylaw #81 appointed a license inspector.

On facing page — The County Gaol which has been standing since before Confederation (from a watercolor by Gordon C. Payne).

This page, left — A birdseye view of part of Woodstock taken from the tower of Old Knox Church in 1865. You are looking north from Elgin and Perry Sts. and can see Simcoe St., Brock St., Dundas St., and in the distance the Old Court House. Many of the buildings seen are still standing. Above, right — This was Woodstock's Wood Market in 1861. It was held one day a week on Finkle St. beside the Town Hall. An auction sale can be seen in progress and in the lower right, Christmas trees.

The town did not possess a lock-up and it was necessary to take any offenders to the County gaol. If charged with being drunk they were allowed time to sleep it off and then brought before a justice of the peace, fined two shillings six pence, and turned loose. The city treasurer received the payment of fines.

The council of 1858 passed Bylaw #82 on February 23, suppressing all drinking and gambling. The saloon keepers retaliated by applying for an "ordinary license". This meant that their establishment became an oyster saloon, a fifty-fifty proposition, one drink with one oyster.

40

A town lock-up was authorized on May 13, 1865, and Wm. Currie was appointed chief constable. He held the position for two months and for the next twenty years, every time council changed, so did the position of chief constable. In fact until 1901, Woodstock had a unique reputation for hiring and firing its staff of peace officers.

The town lock-up was located in the basement of the town hall. The basement contained the furnace and a series of cages which served as the cells. Entrance was gained through a door beside the front steps. The town was not bothered with many drunks but their places had been taken by hobos travelling through town. This basement location proved warm in winter and cool in summer.

Many men have served on the police force of the town but few have gained the respect of Marsh Anderson and his dog Seeker.

The regular force would cease to operate after the day shift was completed. At dusk, Marsh took over. Originally, he was hired as a night watchman by the merchants, but his acts in the line of duty covered all phases of police work encountered during the hours of darkness.

Marsh, as he was best known, was a big man and moved in a manner becoming a man of negro origin. He was followed, as he made his way along the streets, by Seeker, his great dane dog, which could almost be called his shadow. The dog would stand and wait while Marsh tried the doors and peered inside. If there was an indication of trouble he would open the door and let Seeker in to investigate and if needed, he would follow and make the arrest. The trips down the alleys were travelled in reverse. Seeker would lead the way, and as Marsh opened the gates into the enclosures behind the stores, Seeker would enter and prowl around the packing cases and debris. If anything unusual was found, Seeker would utter a deep growl and stand guard until Marsh and his gas lamp arrived to investigate. If a hobo was found sleeping in one of the crates he would be dug out and placed in the lock-up for the night. The procedure followed here was Marsh in front, then the culprit and Seeker bringing up the rear. They never lost a prisoner. Come the dawn, the overnight lodger would be turned loose and ordered out of town.

The duty of the day staff was chiefly dealing with domestic mat-

Above, left — Sheriff Carroll. Right — Dr. Turquand, respected and beloved by all who knew him. He practised medicine for many years in Woodstock while it was still a town.
On facing page — Top, left — The Old Market Building as it was in the 1860's. Bottom, left — This "Sarsaparilla & Lemon" vendor (note the spelling) believed to be a Jas. Izzard, sold his wares on the streets of Woodstock in 1867. Right photo — Marshall Anderson, Town Constable and Night Watchman for over twenty years.

ters. Occasionally a minor outbreak of petty larceny would be brought to their attention. Chief Willis, one of the many chief constables, when questioned by the press as to his intentions, would issue a statement claiming that prompt and vigorous action would be taken by the force. This resulted in the two day constables being nicknamed "Prompt" and "Vigorous". Despite the ridicule, the police force did maintain law and order in its own simple way.

On facing page — Woodstock, from its inception to this day, has been known for its agricultural prowess. Here are four "agricultural" scenes that took place in the days of Woodstock, the Town. Upper left — A scene from 1857 in the Caister Hotel stock yards located on Dundas St. near the present Paquette Hosiery. A lively cattle auction is in progress. Lower left — Prize cattle shown at the Fat Cattle Club Show held on Dec. 12, 1883, in the Town Hall Square. Upper and Lower right — Two scenes from the 1890's taken in front of the "new" Market Building.

On this page — The Town of Woodstock was well populated with tradesmen of all types. Here are but a few. Upper right shows the interior of Sid Coppins' Plumbing & Gass Fitting (note spelling) Shop in which, in 1895, he offered this modern equipment for sale. Above is Mr. Coppins and his plumber's helper, Walter Ramsey, with some of the tools of their trade. Lower right are stonemasons Gracey and Mackay with their helpers as they posed in front of their shop in 1895. The shop was located on the site of the present Federal Building.

FIRE DEPARTMENT

The police force had a counterpart in the fire department and while appearing crude they also performed a duty and earned the respect of the townspeople.

The early fire hall was located at the rear of the town hall. The equipment consisted of one horse, one fire cart and a driver who was on duty to answer a call at anytime.

One of the best remembered horses to pull the little two-wheeled cart was "Farmer", a big brown steed who appeared to be in his delight when he was racing down the street to a fire with the crowds following. Of course, Mr. Kenny was just as pleased as he sat on the driver's seat perched above the drum around which the hose was wound.

In conjunction with the fire department, there were two bell towers, one located in the east and one in the west section of the town. In case of fire the procedure to follow was to run to the nearest bell tower calling out "Fire" as you ran. At the tower you would grasp the rope and pull. This in turn would ring the bell and as if by magic Farmer and company would streak into action. Of course, if the fire was in the heart of town, you simply ran to the station and delivered the message. It was necessary to make sure that somebody stayed at the bell to direct the fire department to the scene of the fire.

Once at the fire two courses of action were possible. If the fire was within hose length of a hydrant the fire was dealt with directly, while if beyond, a bucket brigade had to be formed and the leather buckets that hung on the side of the cart would be brought into action.

Originally it was all bucket brigade until James Hay, the father of the late T. L. Hay, decided that his furniture company needed fire protection and he installed the necessary equipment. He also made it possible for the town's business section to have a water supply to fight fires, and to keep down the dust during a summer drought.

On the right is the old Fire House which was located on the south side of Dundas St. between Victoria and Bay Sts.

Fire departments have, from the beginning, come under the scrutiny of certain citizens who felt that they had too much idle time and were therefore wasting the taxpayers' money. In order to overcome some of the criticism, Mr. Kenny and Farmer, during the summer months, hooked up the town sprinkler and made their way along Dundas and other main streets sprinkling water on the dusty thoroughfare.

One day a lanky negro boy wandered into town and attached himself to the fire department. He spent his time caring for Farmer and doing odd jobs around the station, all without pay. Mr. Kenny, being relieved of these chores, was able to spend his time on more important matters and to show his appreciation moved a cot into the station for the lad. The boy was a likeable sort and the chef at the neighbouring O'Neill House (The Oxford) supplied him with his meals. He was able to pick up his spending money by operating a shoe shine stand outside of the station. Like the others, his biggest thrill was to be seated alongside Mr. Kenny racing to a fire.

On this page — The "new" Woodstock Fire Hall with "modern" fire apparatus ready to roll.

On preceding page — The Woodstock Fire Brigade in 1894. Some people mentioned elsewhere in this book may be recognized. Second and third from the left, standing, are Marsh Anderson and General E. Grant. Third from the right is B. J. Rae who later operated a printing establishment which still later became Commercial Print-Craft Ltd.

WATER WORKS

An essential part of any home was the family pump. This was used to pump the family water supply from a hole in the ground known as a dug well. Originally this was a good service but as the distance between homes narrowed and the now long gone privy increased in number, the family pump became a source of contamination as the surface water became polluted. This led to frequent epidemics of typhoid fever. The town was not capable of dealing with these epidemics so the question came up as how to prevent them. A better water supply was the only solution, but what about the cost? James Hay was a man of great foresight and could see the benefits outweighing the cost and so began his own waterworks department, chiefly for fire protection in his furniture factory.

His offer to supply part of the town with water from his plant on Main St. was favourably received by the town fathers. An agreement was signed in 1880 to purchase water with the option of purchasing the system within ten years for the sum of $25,000. The enterprise proved successful and from the experience gained, the town was able to develop a very successful waterworks system.

In 1885 the first Water Commission was formed by the town council and the present water system inaugurated. The following years saw the townsfolk realize how important a good water supply was.

The original source of supply was Cedar Creek but as it was not entirely satisfactory it was decided to seek a suitable source elsewhere.

In 1890 the first set of springs was purchased from M. Harton of East Oxford, which was followed by the purchase of the Thornton spring on the Sweaburg Road. The same year a bylaw was passed and a forty-year debenture was issued for $105,000, the money being used to build the present plant and purchase more springs which would supply the many extensions to the already laid mains.

On the right is the Woodstock Gas Company's Works (top) and the Woodstock Water Works (bottom) as they appeared in 1899.

With the completion of this major development the citizens of Woodstock secured their first supply of pure spring water through the water mains. The following year the first water commission was elected with the following being the elected members: Mayor Malcolm Douglas, chairman, James Sutherland, M.P., and D. W. Karn. In their annual report of December 1892 they reported 513 services in use and slightly over 13 miles of water mains.

During the next fifteen years, steady progress was made with no section of the city being without a water main. As the mains were extended the citizens were forced to discontinue using water from dug wells. Many claimed that this was an infringement on private rights but slowly they were won over and the dreaded threat of further typhoid epidemics was eliminated.

ELECTRICITY

The use of electric power dates back to the '80s when the first municipal electricity was made at the Main and Mill Sts. waterworks. A limited number of business establishments were supplied. This remained the source of electricity until a new plant was erected. In 1891 the plant was acquired by the firm of Patrick and Powell who also operated the Woodstock Gas Company on Young St. A new building was erected adjoining the gas plant and as new improvements were discovered in the field of electricity they were introducd into the system. J. G. Archibald was in charge of making many

On facing page — This is "Southview", the residence at 269 Light St. of A. S. Ball. This picture, taken in June, 1890, is interesting for several reasons. Notice the hitching posts, the plank sidewalks and the pipes for the new water main which was laid past this home in the summer of that year.

of these improvements. When the town became a city one of the first major acts was to purchase the electric lighting plant and move it to the waterworks plant.

During the early days of the electric system being available to the public, the hours of service were limited. Each evening at 11:50 p.m. the lights would flick off and then on. This was a warning that if you wanted to stay up you had better get out the oil lamp because in ten minutes the power would be turned off until morning. This was not considered a hardship, as the day of radios and television were still in the future and people retired early and enjoyed a good night's sleep.

Like the introduction of a municipal water system, many people balked at the use of electricity. They claimed it was the work of the devil and evil would befall any who ventured to use it.

One of the staunchest dissenters against the use of this product of the devil was a local minister often referred to as "Spitting Billie". This name was given him because of his habit of discharging saliva over his listeners who were in close contact with him. Spitting Billie made it a point to deal with the evils of the devil at every opportunity and warned his followers that if they strayed for a moment, Satan would pounce upon them and their lives would be ruined.

He received a welcome testimony on the devil and his work with electricity one day from a very excited old lady. When the poles had been set along the street and the wire strung, the poles made good spots to tie the local delivery horse while a delivery was being made. As the horse waited it would chew at the pole and spoil its appearance, which resulted in metal plates being put on the poles to stop this defacing.

The day in question was a wet day and the day of good insulators was yet to come. A certain delivery boy tied his horse to a pole, leaving the horse standing in a puddle of water. As the boy made his delivery the horse rubbed his nose along the plate and received a sudden shock of electricity. Becoming alarmed he bolted and left the wagon on the spot just as the dear old lady was passing. This was surely the work of Satan.

The early type of street light consisted of two carbon sticks which, when the power was turned on, would glow as they heated and gave off a light brighter than the gas lamp they replaced. Bob Kerr, who had been the town lamplighter, was responsible for keeping the lights in running order.

Another chore that required continuous attention was the care and maintenance of the wooden sidewalks. The Dundas St. walk was made of 12-foot planks spiked to sleepers below. The other streets had narrow four-foot walks but wide or narrow, they all had the same fault which was that the securing spikes would continually work their way out and could cause a bad fall for anyone tripping over them, especially if they were wearing a long skirt. In order to prevent this happening, the town detailed one of its growing number of employees to patrol the sidewalk armed with a sledge hammer to drive in any erring spikes.

This has been a look into the affairs that had to be dealt with by the town council when Woodstock was a town, and any who wished to dabble in politics had to be prepared to deal with his constituents on these and numerous other subjects.

The pictures on these two pages show parts of Dundas St. shortly after electricity was made available to Woodstonians.

On facing page — Dundas St. (looking east from Light St.) was muddy, had no electric street lights but was well wired in 1898. It did have concrete sidewalks, however.

On this page — Top — This is the corner of Light and Dundas Sts. looking west in 1898. Notice the steel-wrapped hydro poles (to keep horses from gnawing) and the ornate sign on the Opera House (now the Capitol Theatre). Bottom — The corner of Riddell and Dundas Sts. looking west in the same year. One can see the street water tap (bottom right) which was used to fill the Town's steam roller and water wagon. In both these photos the old street corner gas lights can be seen.

THE WAY THEY DRESSED

On facing page — A beautiful bride, a nervous groom, a restless flower girl, bonnets, beards, bustles and braid are all evident in this 1904 photo.

Below is the student body of Victoria School (the West End School) in 1895. "Happy" faces, top knots, lace-up boots on both boys and girls and long curls on some boys are not too different from some school fashions of today.

This page — These are family photos found in old albums. On the left is the Coppins family as it appeared on July 8th, 1887. Strong, rugged and hard-working, families like this were the backbone of the industrial growth of Woodstock. On the right is the Wilsdon family in 1893, dressed in their "Sunday best".

On facing page — The Woodstock General Hospital Graduation Tea of 1899 or 1900 (date not verified) shows the graduates and their guests on the west lawn at the corner of Riddell and Brant Sts. Few smiles are evident in photos of this type because the photographer usually took at least twenty minutes to get his subjects in place.

54

On facing page — Pictures of children and young people such as these (all are from Woodstock) are always interesting to examine. Top row, left to right — A tintype from the early 1850's; taken in 1883; a family group in 1866; two brothers, photographed in 1881. Bottom row, left to right — Photographed in 1883; brothers and sisters in 1889; skipping rope and high-buttoned shoes in 1897; two more brothers in 1900.

This page, below, left — A lovely old grandmother in 1875. Below, right — High fashion, 1850. Upper right — An afternoon chat on Dundas Street, 1900. Lower right — The proper dress for a leisurely afternoon canoe ride on the Thames, 1907.

On facing page — Upper left shows men's casual attire during an afternoon at the Woodstock Gun Club in 1885. Lower left is the student body of the Woodstock Business College in the fall of 1918. Within easy reach by railroad (remaining photo) was Port Dover. Many Woodstonians, like these, found it an ideal camping site in 1884.

On this page — Below is Class 1A at the Woodstock Collegiate in 1919. Faces familiar to many will be recognized. Upper right — All bundled up in a bear rug and ready for a brisk ride in a cutter. These Woodstonians were snapped in 1888 or 1889. Lower right — Although fashions and frills were prevalent in many areas of Woodstock in 1881, this old couple's life revolved around long, hard honest work. Life was difficult for many, and Sunday was the only day on which "good" clothes were worn.

THE IRON HORSE COMES TO TOWN

"There she comes!" This call, which echoed through Woodstock shortly after 12 o'clock noon December 15, 1853, announced the arrival of the first steam-driven train to arrive on the lines of the Great Western Railway. This was a highlight in the early history of Woodstock.

Early in 1832, meetings were held in communities located along the proposed right-of-way between Niagara and London to create an interest and financial support. A charter was granted to build the "London and Gore R. R.". This was extended to Windsor and in 1843 the name "Great Western Railway" was adopted.

Due to the lack of sufficient Canadian funds Francis Hinks (later Sir Francis Hinks) went to England and raised the necessary capital. Work officially commenced on October 23, 1847, with Col. Thos. Talbot turning the first sod. The first train from Hamilton to London, consisting of four passenger cars and one baggage car, left Hamilton on the morning of December 15, 1853.

Each community staged gala celebrations as the train rolled westward. The greatest of all celebrations were held at Woodstock. This was a man's day and as a result the ladies viewed the festivities from behind draped windows. The male population began to gather early in hopes of being in position to be first to see the smoke on the horizon. By noon the excitement had reached a fever pitch and to stimulate extra energy a supply of sandwiches and liquid refreshments were available on the station platform. This is presumably the only time champagne was openly served at this station.

Shortly after noon a puff of smoke appeared on the skyline and a mighty roar went up. "There she comes!" and a small engine with an oversize stack puffed into view. It was gaily decorated with flags and bunting as were the coaches which carried dignitaries picked up along the route. An official welcome was extended by Woodstock's dignitaries and they also climbed aboard and continued on to London. Despite the hilarious celebrating the trip was made from Hamilton to London without a mishap.

On facing page — The Great Western Railway Station in 1866. This station was situated on the north side of the railway track, some distance east of the present station. The picture shows the station master's residence to the right, the 65-ft. flag pole to the left, Henry Parker's wheat storehouse on the extreme left and the third, narrow gauge rail (see text). Above is the "Earthquake", a Manchester-built locomotive which passed through Woodstock many times before being scrapped in 1903. Below is Grand Trunk locomotive No. 40, a Mogul type, which was the first locomotive to pass through Woodstock after the conversion to standard gauge.

On facing page — The Great Western Railway in 1866 just after crews laid the third or narrow gauge rail. Notice that the cars are wide gauge G.W.R. moving stock. The picture was taken from the Finkle Street bridge looking west. To the right are the Great Western mills (later, the Woodstock Cereal Co. and now the Ralston Purina Co. mills); the old Woollen Mills, afterwards the Woodstock Bicycle factory, in the centre; and in the upper left are the Nellis and Maynard residences. Below is the G.W.R. locomotive "Scotia" with the N.G. sign (see text) on her cow-catcher. Upper right is the Grand Trunk Railway station as it appeared in 1899. Lower right is the Canadian Pacific Railway station as it was in 1912.

The arrival at London saw 350 men disembark and proceed to the Royal Exchange Hotel where a giant stag party was held. This was perhaps the biggest affair of its kind ever to be held in London at that time. The less said about it the better.

How did this event affect Woodstock? The arrival of the railroad was a boom to "The Town Plot". Prices began to rise and demand soon exceeded supplies as everybody was anxious to become part of the boom. Men set their own rates of pay and were readily employed or went elsewhere to work. Contractors could not build buildings fast enough and tenants were waiting, some in hopes that a vacancy would occur. Building lots were bringing from 25 to 40 pounds per foot of frontage. To help fill the demand for labor, Irish and European laborers were brought to Canada. There was never a dull moment when these men came to town.

This was only the beginning. The line was extended to Windsor with the first train making the run on January 17, 1854, pulling twenty-four cars on the 220-mile run. Gradually connections were made for those who wished to travel beyond the end of the line. Those going east could make connection at Niagara for points in the United States as well as to Eastern Canada. Those wishing to go to Chicago or west could make connections at Windsor for travel by rail or by steamer. In 1866 a train ferry was launched at Windsor, making it possible to cross the Detroit River without disembarking.

A second line was keeping pace with the Great Western and in order that both would survive the boom the Grand Trunk and the Great Western amalgamated, becoming the Grand Trunk and eventually the C.N.R. During the early days of railroading a milestone was reached when three trains each way passed through Woodstock daily.

The interlocking of Canadian and American Lines was not visualized by the founders of their lines in the two countries. When the Canadian Government was approached for financial aid it stipulated that the gauge for the road would have to be 5'-6", which was agreeable with all concerned. In the meantime, the gauge for American lines was 4'-8½". This was not a major obstacle as there was

Credit Valley Railway

Running in Connection with Port Dover Railway.

NO. 2   TIME TABLE   NO. 2.

Taking effect Monday. 9th September, 1878.

Miles	GOING EAST. No.1. No.3. A.M. P.M.		STATIONS.	GOING WEST. No.3 No.4 A.M. P.M.	Miles
0	7.40 4.00	Dep.	Ingersoll. Arr.	9.15 5.25	10
2	7.45 4.05		× Centreville.	9.10 5.20	8
5	7.55 4.15		Beachville.	9.00 5.10	5
10	8.10 4.30		Woodstock.	8.45 4.55	0
—	8.15 4.35	Arr.	Woodstock, P.D.& L.H.R'y. Dep.	8.40 4.50	

× Flag Station—Will stop on signal.

September, 1878.

G. LAIDLAW,
Managing Director.

not an excessive amount of interchange and it was possible to transfer the cargo from a Canadian car to an American one at the border. Then came the American Civil War and it was considered healthier to deliver goods westward by way of Canada and a considerable tonnage of American goods travelled between Boston and Chicago

---

via Canada. This did create a major problem, especially at the borders.

The year 1866 saw work gangs again laying track. This time they were laying a third rail strictly to accommodate the U.S. rolling stock. This was the answer to transhipping cargoes at the border. Now it was possible to load a car in Canada and deliver it to New Orleans providing it was loaded in a narrow gauge car. As a guide to the switchmen and dispatchers the letter N.G. or W.G. appeared on the cow catchers of the engine to avoid a calamity. This third rail was a real asset to people travelling in the recently introduced Pullman sleeper cars. It was no longer necessary to be awakened in the middle of the night to change cars. Now a person could board a train and retire for the night and get a good night's sleep, arriving at his destination completely rested.

Other lines soon followed the Great Western into Woodstock. The Credit Valley line was started in 1875 and was intended to serve between Toronto and St. Thomas. Work was started at both ends and the two crews joined forces between Woodstock and Innerkip. This line became operational in 1879. In their desire to have a railroad serving the communities in their township many councils voted a bonus to the line if it would enter their township. A good example of this was in East Zorra. The council offered a bonus and in order to get this bonus the Credit Valley R. R. crossed the river which formed the boundary and erected a station just inside the boundary at Innerkip. In 1883 this line became the C.P.R.

Another line serving Woodstock was the Lake Huron and Port Dover Railroad. It was operational in 1875 and served such communities as Hawtrey, Otterville, Norwich, Curries Crossing, Hickson and Tavistock. The C.N.R. took over this line and service to the south ceased in 1941 with a limited service to Hickson continuing until 1964.

Both main lines serving Woodstock ran branch lines to most communities in the county and surrounding areas. The last of these lines is operated between Woodstock and Port Burwell, also a line to St. Marys.

On facing page — On November 16th, 1906, an eastbound Grand Trunk passenger train was involved in a serious derailment as it crossed the diamond just west of Ingersoll Rd. The two top and lower left photos show the wreck as it appeared several hours later. As can be seen, Ingersoll Rd. was poorly gravelled at the time. The crossing guard's shanty and the old signal tower can be seen as can an ancient "privy". The locomotive in the upper right photo is a Mogul type. The lower right photo shows a train wreck on the Canadian Pacific line which occurred just east of Vansittart Ave. in 1907.

The three photos on this page were printed from the original glass negatives. The black areas around the edges of the pictures are simply the effect of age on these negatives. Upper left shows the signal tower at the diamond on the Canadian Pacific line where the Grand Trunk line crossed (originally the Lake Huron and Port Dover Railroad). The tower was located just north of Tecumseh and Brant Sts. In the lower left is seen a beautiful example of a powerful Mogul type Grand Trunk locomotive as it appeared in 1896 while standing in the yards in Woodstock. Above is a photo of the speedy parcel and baggage delivery both railroads offered to Woodstonians about 1895.

GREAT WESTERN RAIL ROAD COMPANY.

Pursuant to the public notice, a meeting of the Stockholders in the Great Western Railroad, was held at the Court House in this city, on Monday the 7th inst., for the purpose of electing seven persons as Directors of the said Company, for the ensuing year.

James Hamilton, Esq., M. D., was called to the chair, and Mr. J. T. Gilkison requested to act as Secretary.

The Secretary read the report of the retiring Directors, after which it was moved by W. A. Harvey, Esq., and seconded by J. Young, Esq.

Resolved,—That the Report of the President and Directors which has just been read, be adopted, and that the thanks of this meeting are due, and are hereby given to them, for the manner in which they have conducted the affairs of this Company during the past year.

Moved by J. O. Hatt, Esq., seconded by B. Babington, Esq.,

That George Notman and Richard Martin, Esquires, be requested to act as Scrutineers.

(Signed,)   JAMES HAMILTON.
Chairman.

Hamilton, June 7, 1847.

The election of Directors was then proceeded with, and the following gentlemen duly chosen :

Sir Allan McNab, ot Dundurn,
George S. Tiffany, of Hamilton,
John O. Hatt,   do
Peter Carroll,   do
Robert W. Harris,   do
Henry McKinstry,   do
James Hamilton, of West Flomboro'.

We, the undersigned, declare the above named gentlemen duly elected as Directors of the Great Western Railroad Company.

(Signed,)   GEORGE NOTMAN,
RICHARD MARTIN,
Scrutineers.

(Signed,)   J. T. GILKISON,
Secretary.

COURT HOUSE,
Hamilton,—June 7, 1847.

REPORT.
To the Stockholders of the Great Western Railroad :

The Board of Directors, whose term of Office expires this day, beg leave to report:

That during the past year, they have used their best endeavors to place the work in that state of forwardness which its great importance – to the Shareholders, to the whole Province, and to the adjoining States of New York and Michigan deserves ; and although its progress has been much retarded by the unprecedented depression in the money market of Great Britain, still they have during the past three months been placed in a position to proceed with the surveys vigorously ; and there are at this time eight full and competent surveying parties, with the necessary office draftsmen, numbering over one hundred persons, actively employed ; which force, is considered sufficient to have maps, plans and estimates, completed by the middle of August next, when the entire line of road will be ready to place under contract. And to facilitate further this desirable object, the Board have already employed competent parties to obtain the right of way on the different routes surveyed.

The Directors are gratified in being able to inform the Stockholders, that their engineer reports, from actual survey, a far more favorable line than the most sanguine could have anticipated. The distance between the Niagara frontier and this city, being only forty-two miles, and the grades are most favorable, the ascent in no instance will exceed 29½ feet to the mile. The line through from the Niagara River to Windsor [opposite Detroit] is found to be 288 miles, being less than any road yet surveyed or estimated on between those points,— and the grades west of Hamilton are likewise very favorable, the heaviest being in this neighborhood, but will not exceed 45 feet to the mile.

The survey will embrace a line from London to Sarnia, which has so far, been found very level, and when the estimates are complete, the Board will be in a position to select the cheapest and best route.

By Order,
J. T. GILKISON,
Secretary.

Great Western Railroad Office, }
Hamilton, Canada, June 7th, 1847. }

Report of the meeting of the Stockholders of the Great Western Railroad Company as it appeared in the Woodstock Herald in June, 1847.

THE PITCHMAN

The Proprietary or Patent Medicine Act of April 1, 1909, removed a character who had become an accepted part of the everyday life of the community. He was the pitchman or sidewalk salesman who travelled from place to place and set up his stall wherever the opportunity presented itself. Usually they specialized in about two items depending on their ability as a salesman. Some would travel with a complete show of their own, which became famous as the travelling Medicine Shows, while others would do a "loner" and perform all characters themselves and also supply their own musical accompaniment.

Woodstock was fortunate in having a Pitchman in permanent residence who not only saved many from an early grave but became a regular feature on Saturday night on the town hall square.

He was a little man with a scraggly beard and wore square lenses in his spectacles. Each Saturday night, Dr. Kinsella, better known as "Doc", would set up his stall on the northwest corner of the town hall square, weather permitting. This stall consisted of a gaily tinselled banner bearing the doctor's name. This would act as a background for the doctor as he stood upon his second piece of equipment, a soap box, and expounded the wonders of his products. The remaining piece of equipment resembled an inverted banjo. This was a lamp, as street lights were not fixtures along the main street at this time. The peculiar part of this lamp was that the oil tank was above the flame and the oil was drained down through a small tube to the burner.

The Doc was of Irish extraction and was possessed with a knack of delivering an endless spiel of Irish wit, which was made doubly enjoyable by his broad Irish brogue. This he used as his come-on to attract the attention of those meandering down the main street on a Saturday evening. Once he had gathered together a group of likeable looking prospects, he would dròp the entertaining and get down to the business of educating them on the wonders of Dr. Kinsella's Elixir of Life Compound. This wonder medicine was made up of a concoction of herbs and tasted like root beer. According to the Doc there was nothing that this wonder medicine could not cure if taken regularly. As a result of his high pressure sales talks he was able to create a market that furnished him with an income to raise and educate a family of respected citizens. Yes, many people claimed that they could not live without it.

This was not his only product for sale. When the gathering had been completely brainwashed and had purchased their supply of the wonder medicine he would then do a second act of entertainment and then present his instant relief to all bothered with tired aching feet due to corns, calluses or bunions. This was Dr. Kinsella's Corn Cure. There was not a corn growing on any man's little toe, or his big one either, that he could not cure. All he requested was that you do not give up faith and continue to apply this wonder of the ages.

With a little final act he would then close up for the night before he ran out of oil, and come next Saturday night he would again be found at the same spot ready to do business in the usual manner.

POSTAL HISTORY

The story of Woodstock's postal history is the story of the growth of the community. As the community prospered, so did the postal facilities. The more progressive the city the more efficient the postal service.

Woodstock, while being designated as a "Town Plot" by Governor John Graves Simcoe in 1792, failed to achieve any status until 1835. During this period the neighbouring community of Beachville was enjoying a short-lived boom, and consequently received post office facilities before Woodstock. Prior to the official opening of a post office at Beachville it was the practice to arrange to have mail left here for settlers in the area, who came to Beachville periodically for provisions.

In the diary of Col. Alexander Light, who settled on the north shore of the Thames, we find that in 1833 it was still necessary to go to Beachville for mail.

During the year 1834 the British aristocracy of Woodstock felt that it was time for Woodstock to have a post office and took steps to procure one. The political problems of that day did not speed the issue and, as a result, the first post office was not an official post office, simply a place to leave and receive mail. It began operations in 1834 and a hand stamp made of hard maple was created. Some early cancels show the grain of the wood in the cancel.

The year 1835 saw the post office at Woodstock officially recognized and J. S. Short officialy appointed as postmaster. The office was located opposite Old St. Paul's Church, Dundas St. Mail was received tri-weekly from London and Brantford by means of a pony express type of delivery by way of the stage road. Jed Jackson was perhaps the most daring of the riders who had contracted to carry the mail.

The contract called for them to carry the mail at the rate of three miles per hour. These men and the stage coaches which followed announced their arrival by sounding their Postal Horn which announced to the community that the mail was arriving and any mail to be dispatched would have to be taken down to the post office immediately. Any mail deposited after the pony express or stage left would be stamped "Too Late" and held over for the next mail.

The official post office produced the second type of postmark used at Woodstock. This was a large two-ring type. Originally, the day of the month was in manuscript and the postmaster was required to write it in. Adhesive stamps hadn't come into existence so it was not necessary to have a "killer", which is a type of canceller that marks the stamp to prevent it from being used again. In place of stamps it was necessary to write and later to stamp the amount of postage required. Mail didn't have to be prepaid unless the sender so desired. If it was prepaid, the amount was written in red ink and if the postage was due it appeared in black.

On January 6, 1841, H. C. Barwick replaced Short as postmaster and the office was moved to a frame building on the east side of Huron Street. The hours were 9 a.m. to 5 p.m. and Sunday 10 to 11 a.m. The rate of postage at this time was charged according to the number of pages being sent. This method had been laid down by the Postal Act of 1765. The rate was $4\frac{1}{2}$ pence currency for a single sheet if the distance to be carried did not exceed 60 miles. Sixty to one hundred miles, 7 pence; one hundred to two hundred miles, 9 pence, and 2 pence per hundred miles beyond.

Letters were termed single, double or treble according to the number of pages. Anything over two pages was treble. All mail for the United Kingdom had to be paid to the port of departure and the remainder was collected from the receiver. Also all mail to the United States had to be paid to the border. Hence the term "Paid to the Line" appeared on letters to or from the U.S.A. All soldiers' and sailors' mail was handled at a flat rate of 1d but had to be signed by the commanding officer. The postage rate was changed on January 4, 1844. This abolished the number of pages and introduced the weight method. The rate established at this time commenced at $\frac{1}{2}$ ounce with a single rate being charged. A single rate being $4\frac{1}{2}$d and was in effect for similar distances as was the number of pages. The rate was raised a single rate for each additional $\frac{1}{2}$ ounce, e.g. 3 ounces was considered as six rates. Letters to the United Kingdom were charged at a flat rate of 1s 4d per half ounce and to the United States a standard rate of $2\frac{1}{2}$d to the border plus the necessary American postage.

A list was published periodically in the British American, a local newspaper, advising the townspeople of letters being held at the post office. This was not a courtesy but a duty of the postmaster, in order to collect the postage due.

The third postmaster, Charles de Blacquiere, was appointed in 1854. The post office was now located at the southwest corner of Dundas and Wellington. The same year saw the introduction of railway mail service between Niagara and London with the mail train stopping at Woodstock. Decimal currency was introduced in 1859, the stamps of that period being classed as the Large Queens.

Woodstock's fourth postmaster was J. C. Vansittart. He was appointed on August 1, 1869, and his death was reported on October 10 of the same year. During his term as postmaster, Woodstock received

Identification of Postmarks — (1) Woodstock's first stamp was cut from a maple block, the date being entered in manuscript. (2) Large two-ring steel stamp with date written by hand. Paid at source postage was written in red to the left of the stamp; if postage was collect, the postmaster wrote the amount in black to the right of the stamp. (3) Great Western Railway steel canceller. (4) Two-ring steel canceller used shortly after Confederation. (5, 6 and 7) Cork cancels. (8) Money order cancel. (9, 10 and 11) Duplex killers unique to Woodstock. (12) Squared circle cancel.

---

its two-ring numeral cancelling device. This canceller consisted of two solid circles with the numeral 23 in the center. All offices were numbered according to their importance. Montreal was #1 and London #6.

The fifth postmaster to be appointed was George Alexander who received his appointment in November, 1869, and carried on as postmaster until his appointment to the Senate as Oxford's first senator on July 15, 1873. The large type Queen stamps were considered impractical and in January, 1870, the now famous "Small Queens" made their appearance. This design became the design that was used

LIST OF LETTERS, REMAINING IN THE WOODSTOCK POST OFFICE, JUNE 4TH, 1847.			
Archibald Robert	Hill David	Edgar William	Phelan John
Bartley O. 4	Holtby Rev. Matthias	Elliott Archibald	Perren Thomas
Ball Wm.	Horan Timothy	Evans Joseph	Palmer George
Beam Henry	Hugal William	Ellison Benjamin	Rouviere Mr.
Beveradge Jacob	Johnson Walter	Finlayson W. D. 2	Ross William
Bloomley Thomas	King Robert	Fraser William	Rice Alfred
Brien Mary	Karn Adam	Fraser Robert	Rickard Martin
Bishop John	Locke W. H.	Forbes Sarah	Sallows Rev. Edward
Braham E.	Luddington Tracey	Farlow A.	Smith George
Burk Hiram	McDonald William	Fresher Robert	Thompson Robert 3
Caister Caleb	McHerren Archy	Frizzel Mrs. 2	Thomson John
Campbel George	McKay James	Fletcher Rev. Charles	Taylor James
Canfield Joel	McKay Neil	Fullock Charles	Taylor William
Coffy Stephen	McKinsey Alexander	Griffith Mrs. Herbert	Tree John B.
Coventry H.	Miller Avery 2	Gunn John	Thimble Jas.
Collins Patrick	Murray James 2	Groves F. J. S.	Vandecar Benjamin
Cook Daniel	Murray John	Grey William	Wilson Augustus
Clark Mr.	Murray Wm. & Robt.	Grice William	Wilson James
Copp John	Meddows Harriet	Gleeson Cornelius	Welford F.
Cotton Henry	Morrison Margaret	Hall William	Waterhouse Joseph
Coventry John	Mattheson John	Hardie J. L.	Whegle Wm. Samuel
Davidson Andrew	Munro Hugh	Hall Valentine 2	Walker Edward
Dean James	Neaves George	Heyland Rev. Mr.	West Edward
Donaley James	Platt William		

Persons calling for the above letters are requested to state that they are advertised.

H. C. BARWICK.
POSTMASTER.

Postmaster's advertisement clipped from the Woodstock Herald, June, 1847.

---

longer than any other. As all offices didn't receive a numeral canceller, the postmasters started creating "killers" of their own. They became famous as the cork cancels. The majority of them were cut from the cork bottle stoppers used at that time. George Alexander, being a mason and needing an extra "killer", created his own and used the Masonic square and compass emblem. Several other offices also used this design. The one created at Woodstock in 1872 was smaller and considered neater than the one at Beachville. All Masonic cancels have now become collectors' items. Later cork cancels used at Woodstock included a Star Burst and a Broken Circle. These were used about 1888. The post office was moved to Perry St., and the coat-of-arms can still be seen there.

The man named to become Woodstock's sixth postmaster was Alexander McCleneghan who served from November 1, 1873, until March 3, 1904. During his term in office many changes took place. The Woodstock office became an official money order office and a canceller marked "Woodstock M.O. Ontario" made its appearance. There is no record of the date it was first used or the last day but it is to be found on letters dated during the year 1881.

A reclassification of post offices now found Woodstock being listed as a #10 office, not according to importance but according to the amount of business transacted. At the same time a duplex killer was introduced. This would kill the stamp and give the name of the point of mailing all with one strike of the hammer. For some unknown reason the staff at Woodstock created an unusual killer that was in use from 1887 until 1891. It was a large oval killer with 7 bars enclosing #10 in a circle. It has the distinction of having fewer but thicker bars than any other known killer. There were three of these killers used. The first one used in 1887 had the #10 in the circle and the month above the date on the date stamp. The second one had no #10 on the killer. This one was used in 1891. The third killer had #10 in the duplex killer but the day of the month appears above the month. It also was in use in 1891.

The now famous Canadian Squared Circle cancellation made its appearance at Woodstock in 1894. No record of the date that it was first used was kept. The earliest known date found with it in use is March 13, 1894, the last known date of its use being October 23, 1899.

The Federal Building was erected on Dundas and Reeve Streets and became the new home of the post office and Customs and Excise Department in 1901.

Woodstock's seventh postmaster was Henry J. Finkle who was appointed postmaster April 6, 1904. The post office continued to keep pace with the growth of the newly-formed city and an automatic

---

Upper photo — The Perry St. Post Office which was closed in 1901. Notice the coat-of-arms above the entrance. Lower photo — The popular Dundas St. Post Office as it appeared during construction in 1901.

cancelling machine was installed, relieving the staff of seven employees of the tedious task of hand cancelling all mail passing through the office. On November 1, 1909, the post office was rated as a semi-staff office. The clerks at this time received $500.00 per year, their hours being from 7 a.m. to 9 p.m. Eight trains served Woodstock with mail each day.

The year 1910 saw Woodstock being used as a distribution center for rural Oxford. The offices of South Zorra, Oxford Centre, Muir, Beaconsfield and Vandecaar all received daily mail service from this office.

The year 1913 saw the beginning of rural mail delivery from Woodstock. Eight routes were formed and this eliminated delivery to all but Oxford Centre.

It was a red letter day for Woodstock on April 11, 1918, when the first carriers started out on their first delivery of mail to the householders of the city. Originally there were eight walks and a parcel post delivery. A Mr. Brown was the first parcel post contractor. Joseph Stevenson was the first parcel post carrier.

To speed up the handling of other than first class mail, pre-cancelled stamps were introduced. Woodstock with its steady increase in revenue was granted permission to use these in 1912. The name Woodstock, Ontario, appeared printed on the face of the stamp along with two cancelling lines. During the year 1930 the name Woodstock, Ontario, was removed and the numerals 4970 appeared. This had become the official number of the Woodstock office. The single set of lines was replaced with a double set. After 1937 when the use of pre-cancelled stamps increased considerably all office distinctions were dropped and the cancelled lines alone remained.

Number eight in the list of postmasters was James R. Steele who was appointed August 4, 1921. During his time Woodstock saw the staff increased to 23 with 10 clerks working inside. During 1941 the wicket hours were reduced and now operated between the hours of 8 a.m. and 7 p.m. Railway mail service was stopped between Woodstock and Embro in 1947 and was replaced by a Motor Vehicle Service. A second Motor Vehicle Service was inaugurated in 1957, serving the communities of Innerkip, Drumbo, Bright and Plattsville.

The ninth postmaster appointed was C. J. Ekins effective December 29, 1953. The tenth and present postmaster, B. B. Hook, was appointed on January 6, 1958.

The city walks now number 15 and wicket hours are from 8 a.m. till 6 p.m., with the office operating on a 24-hour basis. Woodstock now serves as a distributing centre for Motor Vehicle Service for Tillsonburg, Norwich, Princeton, Beachville and adjoining offices.

NEWSPAPERS OF WOODSTOCK

If a community is to be progressive it is essential that it have a good newspaper. This fact was realized by the citizens of Woodstock at an early date and steps were taken to secure the services of a capable person to establish a local paper.

The first newspaper to appear in Woodstock was known as "The Woodstock Herald and Brock District General Advertiser". The first edition was published on June 7, 1840. The editor was George Menzies and Wm. G. Waldie was the publisher. The editor had formerly been with the Niagara Chronicle. In order to help circulate to the greatest number of homes, grain was taken in payment of subscriptions, the rate of which was 11s 3d in town or 16s 6d if received by mail. Advertising rates were strictly cash.

During the intervening one hundred and twenty-seven years, Woodstock has never been without at least one newspaper. At times there have been two and at one time three daily papers.

"The Herald", as it was known locally, continued as a weekly paper under the guidance of George Menzies until his death in 1847. It was one of the few local papers that did not express its editorial policy, politically or otherwise. The Herald did not feature local news on its front page. This was not necessary, as in a community of 160 homes little went on that the neighbours did not know.

THE
WOODSTOCK HERALD,
AND
Brock District Advertiser.

IS PUBLISHED EVERY FRIDAY, IN THE TOWN OF

WOODSTOCK, (CANADA.)

BY

HARRIET MENZIES,
Proprietress.

TERMS—Eleven Shillings and Three Pence per annum, when paid at the end of the year ; or Ten Shillings if a year's subscription be paid in advance.

WOODSTOCK HERALD,

AND

BROCK DISTRICT GENERAL ADVERTISER

TWO DOLLARS AND A ½   [BRITISH CONNECTION, WITH RESPONSIBLE GOVERNMENT.]   PAYABLE IN ADVANCE.

VOLUME 8.   WOODSTOCK, FRIDAY, JUNE 18, 1847.   NUMBER 359.

Our village on Wednesday last was inflicted with a visitation of "Howes's & Co's. United States Circus." A very great deal of most virtuous indignation has been expended on this subject by some of our Brethren of the Press. We cordially agree with much that they have said on the subject. We really do think that while so much distress and want has been brought to our shores that every penny that can be spared, ought to be first applied towards its relief. We know, also, that there are many other objects, useful as well as charitable, on which abstractedly, it would be better that the money of those who have it should be laid out rather than on objects of mere amusement.

Admitting all this, however, we cannot conceive why the poor *Circus folks* have been specially selected as a mark for our contemporaries to run full tilt at ; in their very praiseworthy care of the public morals. In our humble opinion they have been using a two-edged weapon which will cut both ways.—There is a something, we cannot tell what, which is repugnant to certain minds in seeing a fellow creature exhibit himself for money—let the nature of the exhibition be what it will. But there is a something also, in the nature of man which seems to act more generally, and impels him to desire its gratification, by attending Theatres and Circuses, to witness fictitious representations and feats of agility and strength. It is needless to enter further into the why and because of this. It is so—and seeing that it is so, we would be glad to learn why the good folks in the Brock District should not have the opportunity once or twice in the year of indulging that natural, and therefore we say *harmless* propensity—especially when in the nature of things it can only be partaken of occasionally. So far as the present performance is concerned, we can only say that it was, to say the least, respectable as far as outward appearances went. We do not think that the garb of Mrs. Carroll could be one inch more indecent than that of the Opera dancer, *Cerito,* whom we can state, on authority, his Grace the Duke of Wellington nightly, and with his well known punctuality, feels it to be his duty to witness (with spectacles on nose, we presume,) whenever His Most Gracious Queen and mistress, Victoria, thinks fit to honor the show with her presence. We would be glad to hear our fellow labourers of the Press make out to our satisfaction why these things may be done in the green tree with impunity, and cannot be done in the dry without an uncorking of the vials of their concentrated wrath. Have they not (at least some of them) praised and puffed and puffed again the theatrical doings of some wandering play actors from the States. Why make so much distinction between the acknowledged immoral Theatre and that of the exhibition of those to whom " the green plot is the stage, the hawthorn brake their tyring house."

So far as any tendency to riot or disturbance might have displayed itself, the most timerous need not have been alarmed ; a most formidable body of Constables, was, in the evening, around & in the circus, armed with batons—a precaution which has been condemned in no very measured terms by the Inhabitants of the Town. It seems that some rioting took place at the close of the performance in Hamilton, which was probably the cause of these precautionary measures.

INTEMPERANCE AND DEATH.

Last Lord's Day three young men named Wm. McMullin, Peter Malloy, and Patrick Halford, together with the wife of Malloy, went over to the peninsula in a skiff, and spent a considerable part of the day in drinking at the tavern or grocery established there under the auspices of our Corporation. Malloy and Halford became so intoxicated that McM. refused to re-cross with them in the skiff, and returned by the horse-boat, which with the small steamer, affords we regret to say, strong temptations and facilities for the desecration of the Christian day of rest. The other parties crossed in the skiff safely until they reached a point between the end of Small's Wharf and the shore, when the boat upset in about five feet of water, and melancholy to relate, both the men were drowned, (yet one of them when sober, was an expert swimmer,) and the woman was rescued with great difficulty by the activity of a coloured man who witnessed the accident. Both parties were in the prime of life—the one a carpenter, and the other a miller—and one of them (Halford) had but a few days before arrived here from Ireland with his mother, who is now left childless and a stranger in a strange land. The scene was heart-rending when the widow was called to witness the dead body of her only son the support of her old age ; and was rendered more deeply affecting by the innocent playfulness of an infant child of Malloy, patting the clay-cold features of its dead parent, and pronouncing his familiar name, while the mother, half-drunk and half-drowned, was lying in a state of insensibility in an adjoining room. Who are the criminal participators in the untimely death of those men ? The Corporation is criminated by licensing any Grog-Shop or Tavern on the Island, for public convenience requires nothing of the kind : the proprietor of the Tavern is criminated in furnishing the alcoholic poison which first brutalizes and then destroys; all, indeed, who engage in ministering to the vices of Society are in some degree answerable for its crimes. Who can estimate the wretchedness and misery—the amount of disease and crime which annually results from our 200 City Taverns and Grog-Shops ? When will our Legislators, our Judges, and our Magistrates awaken to the importance of giving the weight of their example and influence to stay the progress of this evil by advancing the cause of the Temperance Reformation ? The welfare of Society imperatively demands it.

The citizens of Woodstock, having come from the Old Country, were interested in the affairs of that country and as readers pay the subscription rates only when they get what they want, world news appeared on the front page.

A second newspaper made its appearance in 1842. The first copy reached the street on August 4, 1842. Wm. Walker was the editor and publisher. The following year he sold out to John F. Rodgers. This paper ceased publication on August 29, 1848.

The life of a newspaper was short in the 1800's and competition was keen. The third paper to appear was published on January 28, 1848, as "The Oxford Star and Woodstock Advertiser". The last issue appeared on January 19, 1849. John Allan was the editor and Alex Hay and James Egan were the publishers.

During the next few years newspapers and editors changed like the weather. The "British American" was started by J. G. Vansittart, son of Admiral Vansittart, with the first issue appearing in September 1848. He sold it to Alex McCleneghan who renamed it "The Times" in 1853. When Mr. McCleneghan was appointed postmaster he sold it to A. W. Francis. The Times, a Conservative Journal, was carried on by the Francis family after the untimely death of A. W. Francis in the train disaster at St. George in 1889. In 1898 it was changed from a weekly to a daily until 1902 when competition proved too great and it bowed out in favour of The Express and Sentinel Review. A fire destroyed the building The Times had occupied in December, 1902. It was located at 514 Dundas St. Ministers often tried getting their ideas over to the public via the medium of the press. Rev. W. H. Langdon acted as editor of a weekly know as "The Western Progress" but this paper was very short-lived.

On preceding two pages — "Woodstock Herald" masthead of June 18th, 1847, and news and advertisements as they were presented in that year. On facing page — Advertisements published in the "Times" and the "Sentinel-Review" in 1888, 1889 and 1890.

A weekly newspaper appeared on the streets of Woodstock on January 1, 1854. This paper was to have the good fortune to outlast all others and become the voice of Oxford County. In order to achieve this it was necessary for it to join forces with its competitors. Originally it appeared as "The Sentinel" and Alexander Hay and John McWhinnie joined forces to edit and publish it. The Sentinel remained the property of McWhinnie until 1870 when he sold out his interest to G. R. Pattullo who became editor and publisher. His brother Andrew joined him in 1870.

The "Review" had its beginning in Princeton under the guiding hand of F. G. Gissing. When the Pattullo family gained control of the Sentinel, the Review ceased to operate in Princeton and it moved to Woodstock to become another newspaper seeking the support of the local citizens. Both papers continued to operate as weeklies until 1886 when for business reasons it was decided to merge and become a daily, to be known as "The Sentinel-Review" under Andrew Pattullo.

The Sentinel-Review came into existence on September 11, 1886, and has continued to operate as a daily until the present.

The first quarter century of publishing newspapers saw many changes. Local news had replaced world news in importance. This being a county paper, residents in the outlying communities were anxious to know what their sister communities were doing for excitement. The first issue of the Sentinel-Review as a daily had a front page made up of six columns, four of them being for news and the remainder for advertising. Two and a half of the four columns were for local news. The main story of the day dealt with the Caledonian Society Field Day which took up more than half a column even though all but three paragraphs were given over to the list of prize winners. The about-town column consisting of personals and incidentals occupied about a third of a column.

Ten years later further changes appeared in the make-up of the daily paper. The front page was now divided between large advertisements and news dispatches from outside points. Local news had retreated to the inside pages and a glance at several copies leads one to believe that the local paper was playing up police court items.

Spring Style Changes Not Extreme

OWING to the shortage of dyes and the great demand for wool this year, we are told that there are to be no very important changes in the styles for the coming season. Of course there are a number of style features that are new, but the fundamentals in the fashion world will remain practically the same. This is certainly something which the majority of us will appreciate, as, with some slight alterations, those perfectly good dresses of ours held over from last summer may be put to good use again this year.

waist also is very simply constructed, being trimmed with contrasting material and buttons. Cut in seven sizes, 32, 34, 36, 38, 40, 42 and 44 inches bust measure.
1652.—Girl's Dress. A very pretty little dress could be designed from the model here shown. Striped material, probably white with a black stripe, would look very nice if made in this style with collar, cuffs and wide belt of contrasting material. Black and white is to be greatly worn this season, and is a combination that looks very neat and...

1644 1632 1658 1636 1650 1638 1659 SKIRT

Not only local court cases but spicy cases in the neighbouring courts were reported in great length; the likes of which are not to be found in daily papers today. The sports page was non-existent in 1896. Sports received coverage but was found under local news. In these old issues some amusing articles, although quite serious in their day, are to be found. One of them was the report on the "Zorra Boys' Banquet".

The banquet was to be held in the Opera House. Fifty-eight speakers were allowed ten minutes each to respond to the different toasts. The chairman was allowed twenty minutes for his remarks. This would have accounted for ten hours of oratory. With supper at 7:30 it is presumed they would get home by noon the following day. Actually it never lasted that long but it was necessary for a deputy toastmaster to relieve the official toastmaster at midnight.

The death of A. Pattullo in 1903 saw the Sentinel-Review change hands. It was purchased by W. J. Taylor, then business manager of the Montreal Herald. He formed a company known as The Sentinel Review Co. Ltd., with himself as president and managing director. He continued as publisher until his death in 1932. During his ownership the Sentinel Review was enlarged and improved until it became recognized as one of the leading small city dailies in Canada.

Following his death, the paper was continued by his estate for a few years and was then sold to Allan Holmes of Galt and A. D. McKenzie of Sarnia, who continued the publication under the name of Woodstock Publishers Ltd.

On June 6, 1944, the newspaper was acquired by the Thomson Co. Ltd., the present publishers.

The next ten years saw further changes on the front page, also to the inside pages. Advertising had disappeared from the front page by 1906 and local news was the main feature of this page. Local illustrations had gained in popularity and when R. E. Butler was elected mayor, his portrait occupied the width of two columns. Two and three columns were used for news illustrations. Weddings were considered of importance and received front page billing. The society editor and her page were yet to come. Ingersoll received better coverage as a staff man was in Ingersoll to keep abreast with the news. A farm page appeared in 1906 and local prices were quoted. Live hogs, $6.00; dressed hogs, $8.00; potatoes, 80¢ to $1.00 a bag; chickens, 5¢ - 10¢ a lb.; eggs, 25 - 30¢ a dozen, and butter 27¢ a lb. Another article of local interest that received complete coverage on the front page was dealing with the fact that Scotch whiskey would be costing more to the consumer.

The year 1906 saw the introduction of the sports page. Fred Wilson had his special column "News and Views on Sports".

News of the war took over the front page during the 1914-18 period. On the lighter side "Bringing Up Father" appeared as a daily comic strip.

The Ingersoll Chronicle ceased publication in 1916 and the Sentinel Review became the only daily published in Oxford County. The title now became Woodstock and Ingersoll Sentinel Review. The year 1916 saw the erection of the city hall fountain as a memento to Andrew Pattullo. In his will he had left $1,000 for the erection of a fountain in front of the city hall. He had died in 1903. The year 1920 saw the women's page appearing regularly.

The boom years of the twenties saw many changes in the handling of the news. The big desire was to have the news in the paper as soon as it happened. Radios had been invented and the competition was keen to see who would be first with the news. On the occasion of something outstanding, special editions would be printed. In keeping with this desire a direct wire service was established to bring Canadian Press news from all parts of the world direct to the office of the Sentinel. This was a major advancement.

On facing page — More advertisements from the "Times" and the "Sentinel-Review" from the 1889 era.

The "Times" office at what is now 514 Dundas St., and its "Newsies" in 1901.

The depression came and a second world war. Progress was slow until the late 1940's when the boom once again swept the country. In keeping with the progress of the community the local newspaper made improvements. Canadian Press news is now received on a monitor which can be relayed direct to the automatic linotypes, thus increasing the amount of type that can be set in a day. Photographically, the newspaper today is far superior to anything that was even thought of before the last war. Electronic engraving has speeded production of photographs from the negative to the press. More sensitive film and electronic lighting has made great advances in picture quality possible.

The first newspapers were printed on hand presses. On paper night everybody from the editor to the office boy was pressed into service. Since that time the local papers have been run off on half a dozen or more presses, each an advancement over its predecessor. In 1903, $13,000 was spent for a Cox Duplex press which was the best available at that time. Today it would be a hindrance. The day of hand setting type is gone and in its place we see perforating machines feeding news into automatic linotype machines.

Today in the printing of the daily paper, the press used consists of two sixteen-page units which can operate separately or as a unit. The finished paper rolls off the press at the rate of 25,000 an hour. Approximately 2,500 lbs. of newsprint is used daily and it is possible to get the news onto the street within moments of its happening.

For 74 years after its inception as a daily newspaper, the Sentinel-Review was published at the same location, 382-384 Dundas Street. In May of 1960 it moved to its present location, 16-18 Brock Street. The modern building was especially built to accommodate the growth and future expansion of Oxford's daily newspaper. In the life of this newspaper many people passed through its employment but few left their mark as did Andrew Pattullo.

He had the good fortune of winning the coveted Gilchrist scholarship while attending St. Catharines Collegiate. He took his scholarship at the University of London. Before he was able to complete his course for a bachelor's degree his health broke and he was forced to leave. He then chose the field of journalism for his life's work. He joined his brother in the Woodstock Sentinel and became junior partner in 1875. He obtained control in 1880.

After reaching the top in the field of journalism, by being elected president of the Canadian Press Association for three consecutive years, he branched into politics. The opening created by the retirement of Sir Oliver Mowat allowed him to accept the nomination for the North Oxford riding in the provincial legislature for the Liberal party. He defeated Dr. Adams of Embro and successfully held the riding during the 1898 and 1902 elections. His death in 1903 created a gap in the political and newspaper fields that was not readily filled.

WOODSTOCK 1867

"Woodstock, the Industrial City" was the title given Woodstock when it became a city in 1901. The community had earned this name over the years as the virgin forest was removed and the community emerged. When Canada celebrated Confederation the list of well-established industries related the story of Woodstock's growth.

The immediate area of Oxford was primarily engaged in agriculture and offered a good market for all types of equipment to ease the farmer's burden. The Woodstock Iron Works established in 1842 was a leader in its field and manufactured stoves, threshing machines, plows, cultivators, mill gearing and sheet metalware. The volume of business increased considerably with the arrival of the Great Western Railway in 1853 and by 1867 H. P. Brown, the owner, had installed a 10 horsepower engine and kept 26 men on his payroll.

In competition with Brown was a company headed by D. Paulin which operated the "Vulcan Iron Foundry" whose staff of twenty-five made a complete line of steam engines, cheese vats, and dairy utensils, along with farm equipment and stoves. The introduction of dairy farming had greatly improved the lot of the farmer and the old log cabin was giving way to substantial brick homes and no longer was the hearth on the kitchen fireplace the proper place to cook a meal. A kitchen stove had become a necessity even though the fireplace still had a place in other parts of the house.

The arrival of the iron rails brought more industries to town. Along the right of way several flour, flax, woollen and oatmeal mills sprang up. The largest of these mills was built by James Watson in 1857 at a cost of $40,000. It was made of brick and was five stories high. The foundation measured 80 x 40 feet. The five run of stone was driven by a 60 horsepower engine and turned out 1,000 barrels of flour a week. There was a ready market for this flour along the Eastern seaboard and in Europe. By 1867 Andrew Easton had taken over the mill.

Other mills included the Woodstock Mills owned by T. Clarke and the International Mills operated by Hayes and Collins.

In the east end was located a linseed oil mill which manufactured oil cake. In the west end along the Thames was located a flax mill and rope factory. This was owned by J. H. Brown who was influential in persuading farmers to grow flax as a cash crop. This busy enterprise kept 40 men on its payroll.

Also along the G.T.R. which we find equipped with a third rail to accommodate the cars of both Canadian and American make, we find the oat mill operated by J. Forrest and the woollen mills of D. Penman and Son. In the east we find the Woodstock Brewery which also made use of the grain from Oxford's farms, belonging to S. Collins & Son. The Cedar Creek Oil Refining Co. of George White and Thos. J. Clark produced a very high grade of coal oil. Clark's Barrel Factory located on the corner of Mill and Queen St. supplied employment for 30 men. Wilson's Tannery was located in the western section of town.

The manufacture of soap, potash, candles, brick and tile was controlled by Joseph Close, an enterprise he started in 1854.

As the automobile was yet to come, the manufacturing of buggies and equipment was a thriving industry. Among the leading wagon and buggy makers we find such names as Gardner and Rose who were located on Van. Ave. Wm. Scarff had his shops on the corner of Simcoe and Perry St. Hugh Ross was located on Dundas St. West.

The numerous saddlery shops were operated by John Douglas, who started his shop in 1837, Carryers Saddlery, Harness and Trunk business had been thriving since 1849, and McKay and Bickerton were recent additions to the trade.

For those requiring the aid of a pharmacist the leading manufacturer of prepared medicines was Stack and Revell. This firm prepared a long line of medicines which they claimed would cure all the aches of man and beast. These remedies included Neligan's Worm Candy which was a sure cure for worms, and if one box did not do the trick, then a second sure would. R. Stacks Magical Pain

King was their finest remedy for all aches and pains. It could be taken internally or applied externally. It was an effective cure for a sore throat if taken as a gargle, if rubbed on the head it would cure a headache. A few drops would cure heartburn and a larger dose was ideal for dysentery. It was an excellent liniment for rheumatism, sprains and stiff joints, and would bring immediate relief to burns and scalds.

Barter's Pills would handle what Pain King wouldn't. They were effective for indigestion, dyspepsia and billiousness along with jaundice and liver complaints. They also prepared a complete line of cough medicine, rat poison and itch ointment as well as Mecca Horse Cure, an ideal conditioning powder for animals.

The majority of the local merchants were located in the vicinity of Market Square or Dundas St. and supplied the residents with a complete line of goods equal to that found in the leading stores of New York or London, England. According to their ads, the merchants must have had buyers in these cities just to be able to keep the latest styles in their shops.

The Oxford Permanent Building and Saving Society which today has become the Canada Permanent Mortgage and Trust, catered to the financial wishes of the population and proudly claimed that its head office was located in Woodstock. C. W. Wm. Grey was the president. It had started in 1855.

Of course, the styles did not have to change quite as often as today because even though Woodstock had two newspapers they were only published weekly. There was the Sentinel and the Times and both charged $1.50 a year for the privilege of serving its readers.

In the town management department we find that the town council met every second Monday at the town hall. The mayor was Wm. Grey and H. P. Brown was the reeve. The position of clerk was filled by John Greig and John Brien was chief constable.

The post office was no longer open on Sunday but was open from 8:30 a.m. to 6 p.m. on other days. Two mails arrived and were dispatched both ways each day.

The spiritual requirements of the population were handled by a number of churches. The Roman Catholic Church had not yet been established here but the Presbyterian Church had four churches, one of which conducted its services in Gaelic. The Baptists had a choice of Regular or Free Baptist Churches. The Anglicans had not yet spread their wings and were still confined to one church in the east end of town. A primitive Methodist Church on Peel St. catered to the followers of this faith.

For those interested in the Masonic Order we find that they had three lodges, all meeting at the Masonic Hall on Dundas St. The King Hiram Lodge advertised that they would meet on the Tuesday on or before the full moon. For the followers of William of Orange, there was also a Loyal Orange Association.

In the field of education Woodstock was privileged in having a Grammar (secondary) School, The Canadian Literary Institute and two common schools. The Grammar School was under the capable jurisdiction of Geo. Strauchan and students could receive a thorough education in the fields of classics, mathematics and higher English. At the college one could study for the ministry or receive a complete elementary and secondary education for a very reasonable fee of $28.00 plus board per year. The board was $2.00 for gents and $1.75 for ladies. The elementary schools, of which Woodstock had two, were located at opposite ends of town. One was at Princess and Beale and the other at Hunter and Delatre. Both had been erected in 1853-54 and the teachers in charge were in the east Mr. Archibald and in the west Mr. Dick.

On facing page — This farmhouse is typical of many in the Woodstock area in 1863. Notice the "modern" windmill.

EARLY RELIGIONS

The first record of religious meetings in Oxford County is found in the diary of James Baby, a resident of Sandwich, who travelled from Niagara to Sandwich on several occasions in the early 1800's. He mentions stopping at a Methodist Meeting House at Beachville. Today this is the site of the West Oxford United Church. It was within a mile of this site that the Baptist movement in Oxford had its beginning.

At the home of Solomon Maybee, several Baptists met and laid the foundation of this movement in Oxford and Woodstock. Among those attending we find Zachariah Burtch, Simon Maybee and James Teeple. Later in July, 1820, they met at the home of Peter Teeple and heard a sermon by Elder Fairchild of Townsend and decided to come under the watchful care of each other.

In the fall of 1821 an elder of the Baptist Church of New York State came to Oxford to take up land in Zorra. When it became known that Elder Thos. Tallman was a preacher of the Free Communion Baptist Church he was asked to preach to the local flock. He, being an eloquent speaker, those who heard him requested that he remain among them. He returned to the United States and the following year he again appeared in Oxford.

On April 22, 1822, in a log school at what is now Chapel and Dundas Streets, he formed the first Free Communion Baptist Church. This was the first church in the vicinity of the Town Plot. Nineteen of the twenty-one members had been members of the early Oxford group. They became affiliated with the Free Communion Church of New York State and severed connections with the Townsend group.

This was the only church in the settlement until 1832 when the Methodists began holding meetings and had visits from the saddlebag preachers who travelled through the country. The same year the Presbyterians formed a church in Zorra but it was not until 1834 that a church was begun in Woodstock.

Their first meetings were held at "Dundas Cottage", the home of David White. At irregular intervals this little band of Scots held meetings conducted by Rev. George Murray of Blenheim and Rev. Donald McKenzie of Zorra.

With the coming of Capt. Andrew Drew, R.N., in 1832, came the Anglican element to Woodstock. The story is told that Capt. Drew married late in life and when his wife presented him with a child at 2 a.m. he was so thrilled that he immediately yoked up a pair of oxen and went to a hill at the rear of his property and drew a large stone down to the site of the present "Old St. Paul's Church". This chore completed, he climbed up on the rock and as dawn broke in the east proclaimed in a loud clear voice, "I give this property as a thank-offering for a House of God, and this stone for the first in its foundation." This stone is presumed to be in the foundation of the present tower.

On facing page — Advertisements clipped from the "Woodstock Herald" of July 30th, 1847. The date under the St. Andrews Society advertisement is a misprint in the original ad. The date should read "1847". Above — The Chancel of Old St. Paul's Church about 1852. Right — The original "Gaelic Church" (as it was called on early maps) later called Chalmers Presbyterian Church.

The Baptist Church flourished and in 1836 the school was removed and a frame chapel was erected on its site. The three leaders of this movement included James Harris, Darius Cross and Elder Tallman. They spent considerable time organizing groups throughout the area. The first ordained pastor of the Woodstock Baptist Church was W. H. Langdon who was ordained in 1828 and pastor in 1836, remaining until 1842. Rev. W. H. Langdon became the first Superintendent of Education for Oxford, serving from 1844 - 1851 when the position was abolished.

The first meeting of which a regular record was kept by the Presbyterians in Woodstock was held on March 13, 1837. Following this meeting Sir Francis Bond Head, Governor of Upper Canada, granted a site on Graham St. for a church. In 1838 Rev. Alexander Gale of Hamilton organized the first congregation. A joint call was issued by Stratford and Woodstock to Rev. Daniel Allen of Fortrose, Scotland. On November 21, 1838, he was ordained at Stratford and for two years served both charges two Sabbaths in succession commuting on horseback. He conducted his services in Gaelic much to the delight of his fellow countrymen. Due to ill health he resigned at Woodstock and remained on at Stratford.

Prior to the erection of their own church in 1842 they met at Goodwin's schoolhouse on Dundas St. East. Following the disruption in 1844 the church building became the property of the Church of Scotland and the adherents of the Free Church of Scotland returned to the Goodwin school. They also met in the Weslyn Chapel.

Capt. Drew undertook to erect the Anglican Church on the site of his choosing, neglecting to give the allotted plot in the Town Plot any consideration. He had hoped that by having the church on his property it would give him the advantage for building sites when the main body of English aristocracy arrived. He was a shrewd business man and had considerable trouble with the contractors. Even after the church was built he refused to give up the keys to the Rev. Wm. Bettridge. This resulted in the members of the new congregation erecting a wooden building which they used for several months until an agreement was reached. The agreement allowed the Capt. a specified pew on the northeast corner of the church rent free. This was in the fall of 1834. In 1835 the bell was placed in the tower. This was done very quietly and when it was finally in position the bell was rung and settlers from far and wide came to see the cause of this mysterious sound.

On September 7, 1838, the church and burial grounds were consecrated by the Rt. Rev. Dr. Mountain, Bishop of Quebec, and named St. Paul's Church. The church continued to grow and in 1851 it was decided to enlarge the building by adding two transepts.

Here again trouble arose with Capt. Drew. These additions were going to interfere with his pew and before he would consent to this being changed he demanded that the church pay him the 100 pounds owing him on the original building. This was paid and the additions completed.

Of interest is the fact that this church was once used as a gaol. In it were confined rebels who were taking part in the Rebellion of 1837.

Col. Deeds, the local commanding officer, sent Wm. Grey with 37 men to round up a party of rebels holding out in a patch of slashings. On route he had reason to believe that a certain barn could also be harboring rebels. He entered the barn and began to probe the haymow with his bayonet. A man named Bedford was the result of the probing and he among others was secured in the church for safekeeping. Eventually he was transferred to London for trial. He was tried by court martial and sentenced to be hanged.

On facing page, top left — Old St. Paul's Church behind its ornamental fence and gate in 1898. Lower left — Rev. William Bettridge, first Rector of Old St. Paul's Church. Lower right — Bishop Benjamin Cronyn in 1868. This gentleman was a travelling missionary in Western Ontario, a Rector in London, Rural Dean in Western Ontario, and in 1857 became the first Bishop of the Anglican Diocese of Huron. Right — Old Knox Church which was located on Perry St. at Elgin.

The Presbyterians who had remained true to their original church, "The Free Church of Scotland", had the majority of adherents to Presbyterianism in Woodstock and in 1848 decided to build their own church. A lot on Perry St. was donated by W. C. McLeod and on this site the first Knox Church was erected. The women of the church raised 200 pounds by holding bazaars and festivals. John Douglas also raised considerable funds for the 950-pound structure. Mr. W. C. McLeod donated the church bell which also did duty as the town bell, fire bell and for curfew, along with calling the people to worship in both the old and new (1897) Knox churches. Lord Elgin in 1894 granted Park Lot #4 in the village for use as a burial ground.

WOODSTOCK COLLEGE

Behind every great venture there is a person who gives the venture the necessary drive while they prefer to remain in the shadows. Such was the case with the Woodstock College. The unsung hero of this venture was Archibald Burtch, who along with his wife Jane, became known far and wide for their energy and zeal in the progress of the town.

Archibald Burtch came to Oxford with his parents in 1799, arriving from Brant's Ford following three tedious days of slavish work cutting the way for their oxen and sled through the swamp until they reached the present site of Woodstock's YMCA. The lots were #18 and 19.

In the assessment of 1812 Archibald was assessed for the west half of Lot 19, six acres cleared, one horse and one cow. Later he bought the other half of this lot and erected a frame dwelling. He married the daughter of Squire Teeple. This is considered to be the starting point of the village.

His first wife died in 1824. He then married Jane Blow, who in her 60 years of married life became known throughout the district for her zeal and determination. Their home soon became the stopping place for settlers which taxed their hospitality to the extent that they had to open a tavern in self-defence.

On facing page — The Canadian Literary Institute as it appeared to an unknown artist in 1867. This page — The main buildings of Woodstock College in 1897.

For some time they sold whiskey at 15¢ a gallon, but soon saw the inconsistency of Christian people selling the stuff and discontinued this practice. They did continue to operate a boarding house and during the erection of Old St. Paul's they boarded 14 workers along with the usual transient settlers.

The old boarding house was in use until 1852 at which time the Burtch Homestead was built. It was made of white brick, two stories and perfectly square. The roof was of tin and a large rambling porch served as a welcoming area. This building still stands.

Archibald Burtch, in the interest of promoting Woodstock, gave 10 acres to the Great Western Railway along with a right of way through his property to the Woodstock and Lake Erie Railway. He was deacon of the First Baptist Church for over 40 years, also served as clerk, assessor and collector for the township and was among the first county councillors. He served as a magistrate for the county and always a member of the Reform Party and a great admirer of Francis Hinks who lodged with the Burtches while in Woodstock.

Archibald Burtch died at the age of 80 in January, 1866. His wife, who was known as "Grandma Burtch", died in 1896 at the age of 92.

There had been much discussion among the local Baptists concerning the forming of a school for higher education. Originally this was simply to be a college of a literary nature. This failed to obtain the support of the Baptist Church governing body but discussions at this level continued with the communities of Woodstock, Fonthill and Brantford all seeking official sanction.

It was then decided to add theology to the curriculum and enroll both male and female students. This move was strongly supported by Rev. F. A. Fyfe of the Bond St. Church in Toronto.

Finally the offer put forth by Woodstock was accepted. The land was given by Archibald Burtch and Woodstock guaranteed $16,000 including the site and half the money was to be raised throughout the county.

At the first meeting of the subscribers the name "Canadian Literary Institute" was chosen and this was the first co-educational college formed in Canada. At this meeting in March 1857, Wm. Winter was elected chairman, John Hatch, vice-chairman, James Kintras, treasurer, and E. V. Bodwell of Mount Elgin, secretary.

The cornerstone was laid on June 23, 1857, by Archibald Burtch with Rev. Dr. Ryerson, the minister of education, in attendance. At the time of the building being constructed Canada settled into a recession which severely hampered the fulfilling of the pledges which had been given in good faith by residents of the county. Faced with the project being a failure, Archibald Burtch obtained a mortgage on his house to keep construction going.

The school opened on July 4, 1860, but it only consisted of one flat of dormitories and the first term lasted for six weeks. During the holiday Dr. Fyfe, who had become the first principal, made an all-out effort to raise the necessary funds for the second floor of dormitories.

The fall term opened with 27 students enrolled but their stay was short as during the night of January 8, 1861, the building was destroyed by fire. The Board of Governors had been foresighted enough to arrange ample insurance and were able to collect $8,000 but as all expenses had not been paid a considerable amount was used to settle the debt.

When word of the fire reached Hon. Wm. McMaster, he immediately offered $4,000 providing the balance could be raised. Once again an appeal was sent out and in response a total of $21,000 was pledged. This allowed a new school to be erected the following summer.

In the meantime the school continued to function as the Woodstock Hotel was turned over to the Board of Governors rent free until such time as a new school was erected.

The new school carried out the original program and three departments began to function, the primary, the higher and the theological. The attendance had increased to about 100 students with fees for the primary and higher students being from $20.00 to $28.00 per year. The students of theology were not charged. The classes were about equal with 30 students studying for the ministry.

View from the Northwest Campus

A corner of the Science Classroom

The Workshop of the Manual Training Department

First Flat of the Workshop (Manual Training Department)

The Observatory

View of buildings from the rear, showing their general arrangement

The Chemistry Laboratory

Front View of the Dining Hall and Museum

A section of the College Dining Hall

The interior of the Chapel

After the death of Dr. Fyfe in 1878 his position was split with Prof. Wells taking the literary and Rev. John Torrence taking the theological department. A lady principal was appointed in 1861 with the honor going to Mrs. S. T. Cook. In 1873 a ladies' building was erected and functioned until the Moulton Ladies' College was opened in Toronto in 1888. This brought to an end co-education in Woodstock. The name was changed to Woodstock College in 1883.

The theology department was removed from the college after 1881 when Hon. Wm. McMaster, desiring to have this department located in a more central position, erected at his own expense the Toronto Baptist College. In 1888 he donated nearly a million dollars towards the erection of McMaster University to carry on this work.

This was a severe blow to Woodstock. It continued to operate as a boys' school but the enrollment dropped steadily and eventually closed August 31, 1926. It was attempted to revive the school under Anglican auspices and later as St. Aphonsus Seminary, but both failed. The original buildings were taken down in 1959.

One of the outstanding teachers at Woodstock College was Rev. Newton Wolverton who taught mathematics and after becoming principal set up the first manual training department in Canada. It is fitting that today on the site of the old College, the Woodstock Board of Education has erected College Avenue Secondary School in which considerable vocational training is offered.

THE TOWN MOURNS

Believe it or not but in 1889 certain citizens in Woodstock were trying to have Mayor D. W. Karn removed from office for lack of service. Another element was taking the town into court over a hydro issue.

These issues were among the last items of business discussed by the elected members of Woodstock's town council prior to that fateful train wreck on Wednesday, February 27, 1899, in which three of the councillors were killed and four severely injured.

93

On these two pages are scenes from the disastrous St. George wreck (see text) of February 27th, 1889, in which several members of the Woodstock Town Council were killed.

At this meeting it was decided that a representation from the town should be on hand in Toronto on Thursday, February 28, when the Electric Light Bill was to come before the Legislature. Woodstock was a leading figure in the changeover from gas to electric lights and their presence was considered of the utmost importance.

The delegation consisted of Mayor D. W. Karn, Reeve Francis, Deputies Peacock, Martin and Knight, Councillors Swan, Potts and Jos. Peers, along with Clerk George C. Eden. An invitation had been extended to the following who for different reasons were unable to make the trip: Messrs. J. M. Grant, R. W. Sawtell, Dr. McLay, R. Bird and W. M. O'Breirne. Mr. Sawtell was at the station to see them off and had decided to wait until the following morning before joining them. The party boarded the St. Louis Express, commonly known as the 520 Express going east, and settled down with Clerk Eden and Councillor Potts going to the smoker accompanied by Francis. The first two found seats but when Francis failed to obtain a seat he returned to the car carrying the remainder of the delegates. The train had an uneventful run to St. George but as it approached the bridge east of the station the engineer noticed splinters flying up from the track alongside the engine and a sudden vibration seized the train. It was later learned that this was caused by one of the drivers on the engine breaking free and whirling around at a terrific speed, smashed the timbers on the bridge. Before the calamity had struck, the engine, baggage coach and smoker had successfully crossed the bridge.

The next two coaches were passenger coaches. They left the track, the first one fell crashing to the bottom of the 60-foot canyon while the second car nose-dived straight down, spilling its passengers and baggage into the nose of the car to be buried by the debris which followed. The majority of the passengers in these cars were either killed or seriously injured. The diner, which was next in line, spun crazily around but remained on the bridge approach. The rest of the train remained on the track.

Councillor Potts and Clerk Eden, being in the smoker, immediately made their way to the wreckage and located Messrs. Karn, Knight and Swan lying in one corner of the car. They smashed a window and got them out. They found the body of Reeve Francis lying on the ground and they also located Peacock in a dazed condition in the same car. The Mayor's chief concern was for the safety of the reeve. Mr. Peers was killed instantly and Dr. Swan, whose last words were to the clerk, "Is that you, George. How did you get saved?" died shortly after in the hotel at St. George which had been turned into an emergency hospital to care for the injured.

The news of the accident reached Woodstock shortly after 7 p.m., with word that a relief train was on its way from London. Stopping at Woodstock it took members of the immediate families and doctors, along with members of the local clergy. The injured and bodies of those killed were returned to Woodstock and the town grasped the seriousness of the situation when they began to realize that most of their council were either killed or seriously injured.

The councillors who had remained at home called an emergency meeting and in conjunction with the town's ministers declared Saturday, March 2, 1889, as a day of mourning. They requested that all places of business remain closed and flags be flown at half mast. A combined funeral procession was arranged and as the services were concluded in the different churches the cortege formed up with the others for the procession to the two main cemeteries and then to their respective plots. Dr. Swan, Reeve Francis and Mr. Peers were given full military and Masonic honors.

The loss of Reeve Francis was doubly felt as he was also the editor of the local paper "The Standard". In reporting the accident his newspaper lined the item with heavy black lines.

Following the day of mourning the city observed a further period of mourning by cancelling all public festivities. Mayor Karn remained a cripple for a considerable length of time but eventually recovered.

Incidentally the Electric Light Bill was passed and Woodstock was one of the first to sign it.

On facing page — The interior of the Bain Wagon Works Fire Station in 1895. Notice the telephone on the left.

THE TELEPHONE COMES TO TOWN

Woodstock first became acquainted with the Bell family in 1868 when Prof. Alex Bell, the father of the inventor of the telephone, and his brother David, while vacationing in Canada and the United States, were invited to Woodstock to give one of their famous evenings of entertainment. They shared a distinguished reputation as specialists of speech and elocution. The gathering was not large but they thrilled their listeners as they read such numbers as "Virginia", a play of Ancient Rome, "An orator's first speech in Parliament", along with more humorous numbers, "Shamus O'Brien" and "Nothing to Wear".

The professor returned to his home in Scotland only to return to Canada with his family in 1870. In 1874 the telephone idea was disclosed by Alexander Graham Bell to his father while the young inventor was vacationing in Brantford. Many experiments followed and in 1876 the first long distance call was made between Brantford and Paris, Ontario. During the experimental period the telegraph lines were used to carry voice and some of the experiments were conducted over the lines in the Woodstock area.

In 1877 a telephone demonstration was conducted between Stratford and Woodstock. This was done during the busy period of the day, but despite interference, the calls were received at Woodstock loud and clear. The instrument in use at that time was declared as quite simple, consisting of a tube of wood about six inches in length and tapering from two inches in diameter down to one inch. Inside the hollowed-out tube was a small iron disc called a vibrator which was connected with telegraph wires at both ends. No battery was needed as the unit was complete in itself. The party speaking, spoke into the tube while the receiver put the tube up to his ear. The procedure was reversed when the receiver wished to reply.

It soon became an instrument of great interest. All who saw it classed it as one of the greatest inventions of the 19th century, and forecast a great future for it. An experimental unit was set up in Woodstock operating between the Dominion Telegraph Office and Stark and Revell's Drug Store.

Robert Stark became very interested in the telephone and came up with an invention of his own, a telephone cable which would eliminate the need of moving the telephone while speaking. It was not put into use but he was made the first telephone manager in Woodstock when a telephone office was opened here in 1878 by the Dominion Telegraph Co., who were appointed agents for the Bell Telephone in Canada in 1879. This office served six telephones on two lines.

Telephones were leased to John Forrest and James Hay in March, 1879. Mr. Hay rented three units, one for his home and two for his furniture factory. Forrest had two units with one at his mill and one at the telegraph office.

The name McCleneghan enters the picture in 1879 when he was appointed manager, replacing Mr. Stark. While manager he arranged a telephonic concert between Woodstock and Brantford on Nov. 1 and 12, 1879. On the first concert he arranged to have a Miss St. John of Chicago sing over the telephone from Woodstock. The reception at Brantford was good but the young men seeking an introduction with the young lady apparently became excited and jumbled up their words so that the reception at Woodstock left much to be desired. The second concert featured the voice of Rev. W. W. Carson of Woodstock but formerly of Brantford. The reception both ways was perfect this time.

The steady growth of the telephone in Canada caused the Bell Telephone to take over control of its Canadian interests from the Dominion Telegraph Co. in April, 1880. By this time Woodstock could boast of having twenty-eight telephones in use with fifteen subscribers. By the year's end this list of subscribers had increased to twenty-seven and reached forty-three in 1883. The office was located on Dundas St. with E. T. Jackson as manager. Hours of business were 8 a.m. to 8 p.m. on week days and Sundays from 2 p.m. to 4 p.m. In the directory issued in 1887 there was a notice stating that the office was always open. The town received its 100th telephone that year.

Prior to 1890 it was a simple matter to place a call. You simply contacted the operator and asked for your party by name and the call would be placed, but due to the large increase in subscribers the idea of giving each telephone a number came into being. The number of subscribers reached 200 by 1895 and 259 by November 1901. The office was moved from 412 to 510 Dundas St.

Following World War I the demand for telephones increased rapidly with the one thousandth telephone being installed in 1919. A new building was erected at 26 Graham St. in 1923, complete with the latest equipment, and the following year battery operated telephones replaced the magneto units.

The demand for telephones continued to grow with the growth of the city and it was realized that a telephone was a necessity and not a novelty. The 2,000 mark was passed in May 1925. To better serve the public, the Bell purchased the independent companies operating in the area. These companies consisted of "The Canadian Independent", "The Pioneer" and "The Excelsior" Rural Telephone Companies.

It is interesting to note that many of the smaller rural companies ran their lines along the farmers' fences and used glass bottles for insulators.

The big change came on November 20, 1954, when Woodstock got the dial system. The cutover from battery to dial was a major undertaking and to house the equipment for this service a special building had to be erected and the familiar sound of "Number Please" was replaced by the dial tone.

The first long distance call was made by Wallace Nesbitt, M.P. for Oxford, to Major General Pearkes, V.C., of Victoria, B.C. The first local call placed on the dial system was made by Warden James Hossack to Mrs. E. Brewster, 147 Delatre St., wife of a former manager of the Bell at Woodstock. The code number now became Lennox 7 which has since been replaced by the numbers 537 or 539 to fit in with the direct dialing service which is gradually being put into service across Canada. The latest figures for the number of units in service as of December, 1966, list 12,152 units in Woodstock and 31,704 units in the area covered by the Woodstock exchange.

VANSITTART AVENUE

Have you ever driven down Vansittart Avenue and gazed at the homes on the avenue and wondered just what tales they could tell? Many interesting yarns would come from them such as the story of the Rose family. Their home has gone to make way for York Knitting Mills as has the building where Mr. Rose had his egg grading plant.

But the Rose girls were known all along the Avenue. They are remembered for the fact that they were named Lily and Violet after flowers. Or maybe the houses could tell about the time young Frank Ball discovered the old Watson house on fire. When he investigated, the windows were too hot to touch. The engine was called out and prevented a major fire that could have destroyed many fine homes on the street.

Seeing that the houses can't talk, let me tell you about this street and what it was like. Van Ave., as it is now commonly called, has always been considered as "the Avenue" and to live on the Avenue was the final step up the social ladder of the elite of Woodstock, at the turn of the century. A glance down the list of residents turns up a fair collection of doctors, lawyers, merchants, gentlemen and town and county officials.

The social standing of these people is quite visible in some of the homes that are still standing. The owners of these homes engaged many servants including gardeners, parlour maids, kitchen help and often, a retired army officer would keep his batman on as his personal servant. Yes, it was something to live on the Avenue.

When we say it was the top of the social ladder in Woodstock, it was also the springboard to greater heights in other localities. George Smith was appointed judge and went to live in Windsor. J. G. Wallace also became a judge but stayed in town. Then there was the Forbes family who operated the Commercial Hotel. They also distinguished themselves with their horses on the race track. When one of the turf men of the family died and returned home for burial it was considered a day of mourning for the town. The local paper of the day carried a series of articles on his life.

Along with this we have a name that is still well remembered due to the fact that their home is still a show place of Woodstock. At present it is known as the St. Joseph Academy. It was built by Thos. L. Willson in 1895. The home was designed by a New York architect and cost $90,000 to build. An outstanding feature of this house is a stained glass window depicting the eighth century Holy Roman Emperor Charlemagne studying under Alcium, the British-born leader of the Emperor's revolutionary educational revival. Carbide Willson, as he was known, earned his fame and fortune in Hamilton and in New Jersey but when it became possible for him to live on the fruits of his labors, he brought his bride of a year to live at 210 Van Ave. Born in Princeton, he was a grandson of Hon. John Willson, one-time Speaker of the Upper Canada Legislature.

Speaking of some of the families we must recall the family of F. R. Ball who served the county as crown attorney. The Ball property was located in the area of the Lion's swimming pool and originally contained five acres. The old home was one of the first to have gas lights. At night the house was lit up from the basement to the attic and folks would walk out there just to admire the lights. F. R. Ball was a very civic-minded citizen. It was through his efforts that the Avenue and Victoria Park were lined with trees. When it was noticed that a tree had died it was immediately replaced. The crown attorney used to delight in walking down the Avenue on his way from the office. A very good friend of his, Squire James Ingersoll, had the adjoining property. Another very good neighbour was Wm. Higgins, simply classed as a gentleman. An interesting story is told about Higgins. He was an English officer in the Peninsular War. At that time the officers' wives travelled with them and among other things did their washing for them. While on parade one day, the Duke of Wellington asked Capt. Higgins who did his washing as his shirt waist was so white and the frills so perfect. When learning who, he inquired if maybe she would do his, to which she consented. A family heirloom was a spoon she received for her trouble. Also the Prince, who later became Edward VII, served in Higgins' company. When he retired, his officers presented him with an engraved silver tray bearing their names.

The Vansittart Avenue children were no different from any others. They knew the choice swimming holes at the river and all attended the same church, as the separate school was not operating at the turn of the century. What is now Central School and the old Collegiate Institute were the seats of learning. Miss Alice White, one of the teachers, resided on the Avenue.

The Patterson Works, which were later taken over by Massey-Harris, were among the most important industries in town, being operated by Peter and James Patterson who lived on the Avenue across from the Ball property. Another important manufacturer was W. C. Stewart, who was general manager of Stewart Manufacturing, recently taken over by Beattys of Fergus, and moved out of town.

Of course, the White family of merchants lived on the Avenue as did the Campbells who operated a drygoods store which later became Walker's first store in Woodstock. Several other merchants including J. M. Whitney, the jeweller; W. W. Lee, confectioner; Mr. Buchanan, the hardware merchant; John Strothers, the carriage maker; John Yeo, a shoemaker, and James Hamilton another hardware merchant, had homes on the Avenue. In the professional services, besides the barristers, we find Dr. A. G. Rice, Dr. Andrew McKay, Mr. Scott, the chemist, and F. Crosby who served as an accountant and later manager of the Bank of Commerce. The insurance firms were represented on the Avenue by R. W. Ball. He was not related to the other Ball family but quite frequently received their mail, including an invitation to a dress ball in the Town Hall. It was wondered at the time why the Crown Attorney did not receive an invitation. Later it was learned that it had been mis-sent and R. W. enjoyed a very delightful evening.

Today as the City incorporates more land within its boundaries, new areas are attracting successful business men. Many are still retaining their place on the Avenue and as long as the palatial homes along the Avenue remain, it will remain one of the show places of Woodstock.

THE TREATMENT OF THE POOR

The following was taken from Some Recollections of
Right Rev. John Cragg Farthing

To my horror, I found that the indigent, houseless poor were given shelter in the County Jail. They had to be formally committed by the Magistrate as vagrants. Of course, one visited them as one would other parishioners, no matter to what communion they belonged. The jailer was very kind, he did not confine them to the cells; but I felt it was a reflection on the whole community. When one of them died we used to give him a decent burial. We arranged for a hearse and the proper care of the body, "commandeered" young men — bank clerks and others — to act as pallbearers. They were most willing to render every possible service and gladly responded. Then we got the local press to write it up, and point out the shame of having those whose only crime was their poverty thus treated. Public opinon was worked up. The County Council finally built a very nice Home for the Poor about two miles out of the town. I used to visit them there, and for some time I held a service there every Sunday after my Sunday Schools — I rode a bicycle to and fro each week. This grievously shocked the Sabbatarian convictions of many Protestants. Quite a large deputation of non-Anglicans called on me and said I was a cause of much scandal by riding my bicycle on Sunday afternoon through the town. I expressed my regret at giving offence, but said "There are fifty to sixty old people at the Refuge. I am the only one at present taking services there each Sunday." (Others helped after some time, going out in rotation.) If I get a horse and buggy and drive out, the livery man works, and the horse works; I have not the time to walk there and back and take my services. If I bicycle, no one works but myself. I can't afford to pay the livery for a horse and buggy every Sunday, as my services there are purely voluntary. If you men, however, will pay the livery stable bill each week, I will gladly drive out." This suggestion seemed effectually to overcome their Sabbatarian scruples! I heard no more from them!

Our Anglican poor residing in the city were well cared for. We could not, however, care for all the poor in the City and County. We had a pretty good Poor Fund which the rector administered, which was a substantial nucleus. Our people were eager to help. In my first year at Christmas time I hired a horse and sleigh and drove round and delivered the Christmas dinners myself. I never did it again. The keen eyes of the neighbours knew who got Christmas dinners, and thoughtless children would twit their playfellows with

The County Jail in 1897.

help as it would to any individual member of our own family. The children, thus privately helped, grow up with a strong attachment to the church, and become throughout their lives active and valued members of the church. My experience confirms this with the happiest results.

The world watches the Church, and individuals exercise a great, and often an unknown, influence. A working man of excellent character brought up in a Protestant Communion, though not then an attendant, was unwell and stayed at home from work. As he was looking out of the window he saw two ladies going into a house opposite, where a very poor woman was seriously ill. A heavy snow storm and blizzard was raging. He afterwards said to me, "The religion that would bring those well-off women all the way down through such a storm to visit a poor woman and her family, must have something in it." The women were Anglicans. The upshot of it was that he was confirmed and became a regular communicant of the church, and one of his sons is now doing excellent work in the ministry of the church. Thus we see the influence of a Christ-like act.

THE BOYS' VESTED CHOIR

The following was taken from Some Recollections of
Right Rev. John Cragg Farthing

it. It was apt to humiliate the family. Thereafter we made private arrangements with our grocer, coalman, and boot and clothing men, and gave the order to the head of the business and he filled it and delivered the order by his regular delivery wagon. This was our rule; seldom was it violated. I felt that the thing to do was to preserve the self-respect of the family. It draws them closer to the church; if their self-respect is not regarded it is apt to alienate. If they are humiliated before their neighbours, they are embittered against the church which materially helped them but spiritually degraded them. Public administration, with its system of investigation by committees, cannot avoid more or less publicity. The Church, as the family of God, can render

I was anxious to get the boys more and more interested in the work of the church. The suggestion that we should have them in the choir and have them vested, was generally warmly supported in the parish. There were then in Western Ontario only three boys' choirs: St. Paul's Cathedral, London; Grace Church, Brantford; and All Saints, Windsor. I found a parishioner keen on having the boys' choir and able to train them — Mr. Hayden, the Grand Trunk Station agent. We had some good men's voices. We could not get boy altos, so we had four ladies who did not join in the procession. The innovation naturally caused discussion through the town, and many Protestants said it was Roman! The boys were keen about it.

On the first Sunday morning that the boys and men marched in robed in cassocks and surplices, I explained to the congregation our reasons for the change. The custom of the Anglican Church was that those who ministered in the church should wear ministering vestments. The choir was officiating before God, leading the praise of His people, therefore it should be suitably vested. This tended to greater reverence and devotion. Every Englishman knows that all cathedrals and most parish churches in England have boys and men vested, to lead their praises to God. Then there is a very practical reason also. Some of the boys may come from poor families, while others come from homes of well-to-do people. This would make the boy with plain clothes feel mortified beside the well dressed boy. Put robes on them and they are all alike. The change was most popular.

We all took great interest in the boys. They played around the church and rectory. In winter I flooded the lawn, and though the rink was not full size they played hockey there. If they were cold my wife let them warm themselves at the kitchen fire. Some people told me that flooding was bad for the lawn. I replied, "Maybe it is, but it is good for the boys, it keeps them around the church." Every summer I took them for two weeks camping on the shores of Lake Erie. There we lived under canvas, had our meals under the trees, had boating, bathing, cricket, baseball, corn roasts, etc. We had a short service morning and evening in the open air. On Sundays the boys were proud to go to the local church and, duly robed, sing at their service, giving them an anthem.

On arriving at the camping site one summer the ground was very wet, and I feared it would be risky to pitch tents. There was an empty cottage which I wanted to rent and keep the boys' bedding dry. It was owned by a man who was named, having been duly baptised as "William Prince of Orange MacCoy"! It was during the United States Spanish War. The old man told me with much positiveness that "them Philippines were the people to whom S. Paul wrote his letter." (Philipians.) I was so anxious to get the cottage I did not discuss it.

Nothing that I ever did in the parish gave me greater spiritual results than the boy choir. Several of the boys took Holy Orders, one is a bishop. Many of them, some for other communions, have been active churchmen throughout their lives. I was perfectly frank about it and told the parents that if they let their boys stay in the choir they would probably turn out Anglicans. One Presbyterian mother said, "I don't care if he is an Anglican or not, as long as he is a good man." That boy has been an earnest worker all his life and is now. Eye trouble prevented him taking Holy Orders. I spent one day in Woodstock last year and I called on him and his wife and had a chat. We have kept in touch with each other through the years. I have tried to follow the lives of the boys as far as possible.

In course of time we had different choirmasters and organists, as the railway moved Mr. Hayden. When the Westminster choir was

touring the United States, Canada, Australia, etc., one of our boys, trained by our organist, Mr. Charles White, who had a fine musical education in England, was heard by the leader of the Westminster choir, who wanted him as a soloist, but his parents would not let him go. Many thought he was superior to their soloist. It showed that Canadian boys can be trained to sing, that our climatic conditions are not prohibitive. May it not be that our Canadian musicians have not had the experience of the English directors? However, the fact remains that in Canada we have some quite good boy choirs; and in England they have quite bad ones too!

A parish which does not utilize its boys in the worship of God is losing a great opportunity. Boys like singing, and when clergy and people take an interest in their lives, the choir will be a fruitful training ground for manhood.

The Woodstock General Hospital in 1897. The "New" Hospital sits majestically on a rise facing south onto Brant St. On the extreme left is "Rossmore", the home of Mr. John Ross Shaw, which is now part of the Hospital complex. At the time this photo was taken, Mr. Shaw's estate extended from Riddell to Graham and from Brant to Vincent St.

THE CARE OF THE SICK - - BUILDING OF THE HOSPITAL

The following was taken from Some Recollections of
Right Rev. John Cragg Farthing

Woodstock was not only the centre of a large and splendid farming community, but it was also an important manufacturing town. There were, therefore, many young men living in boarding houses. Every autumn there was an epidemic of typhoid fever, owing to the bad water supply. The nearest hospital was at Brantford, about thirty miles away; and there was not a trained nurse in the town or vicinity. When a boarder got the fever,, the landlady could not look after him night and day; so we had to get inexperienced people, particularly at night. When the doctor told me that I had the fever, I said, "I must go to the hospital." He said, "That is a grand idea, for then next week we will have a fine big funeral!" I had to telegraph to Toronto, ninety miles away, for a nurse. I was living in rooms, unmarried, at that time. My father and stepmother had gone to Long Island, N.Y., my father having a temporary position there. My good friend Mr. William Grey, the patriarch of our congregation, insisted on my being taken to his house. I collapsed at a service in the church at which he was present.

It was this state of things which caused an ever-increasing demand for a new water supply; and made some of us start an agitation for a local hospital; both of which were essential for the well-being of the people in a town of over nine thousand inhabitants, and the county town of one of the most fertile farming districts in the Province of Ontario.

When they were agitating for a new water supply, public meetings were held. One of our active professional men who was well known, but who was slovenly and careless about his clothes and personal habits, was urging the people to support the new water scheme. Referring to the source of our bad water supply he said, "Why I remember, when a boy, bathing in that stream." A witty lawyer in the hall called out, "That settles the steam" — whereat there was much laughter. After the new water supply came, there was an end of yearly typhoid epidemics.

The building of a hospital became an issue. I took an active part in the campaign. We got some of our business men to serve on a citizens' committee, but one was amazed at the opposition to it. We had three outstanding surgeons, one of whom, Dr. A. Beverley Welford, was particularly keen to have a hospital. He worked with me in visiting neighbouring small hospitals in Brantford, St. Thomas and London, to get information for our guidance in building and equipment, and to get facts which would help us in allaying opposition. Some asserted that our surgeons wanted it so they could cut up their patients! The ministers of two of our large churches opposed it. One urged his people to support the church funds and let the hospital wait; the other said it was not needed, it was just a fad of mine. I had the satisfaction of visiting this good minister at a later date when he became a patient in one of our private wards! I did not remind him of his former opposition. I let his conscience do that! We had the support of our surgeons, Doctors Welford, Sinclair and Park, who wanted it for their surgical work, for which they were widely noted.

We had a public meeting and launched a campaign. It was hard going. Mr. Malcolm Douglas, one of our most trusted business men, manager of the Trust Company, was enthusiastic about it, and canvassed the business community with me. Others also helped in the canvassing. Mr. Douglas' minister was one of those who opposed the hospital. We got considerable financial support from a farmer, Mr. John Whitcher, living in the Niagara peninsula.

On facing page — Woodstock General Hospital in 1902. This building, which has served Woodstock faithfully and continually, night and day, for over seventy years, is about to be razed, a necessary action but a sad loss to our community.

At a critical moment, unexpected help came. We were debating whether we could build or not, and were enquiring about a site, as to suitability and price. Mr. Douglas wrote to Mrs. Warwick in Toronto, a former resident of Woodstock, to know if she would sell some property which she still owned in Woodstock, and how much she would take for it? She replied at once that they had made the beginning of their fortune in Woodstock and, if that property was suitable, she would be delighted to give it as a thank offering. That generous act settled the question to our great joy. The site was ideal. In later years the Hospital Board bought adjoining property, which gave us grounds for a garden, and prevented the possibility of undesirable neighbours.

A small hospital of thirty beds was erected. We had a small operating room which was fairly well equipped. There was a debt on the building, and the strictest economy had to be exercised. I was secretary for several years, and kept the books, going up oftentimes in the evenings. We had a very strong committee — the Hon. James Sutherland, M.P., who later became Minister of Public Works; J. D. Patterson, John White, D. W. Karn, T. H. Parker, Malcolm Douglas and George Eden.

We had Miss Falconer, an exceedingly clever nurse, a graduate of the Toronto General Hospital, as our first Lady Superintendent.

Gradually the hospital grew in public confidence, largely owing to the skill of our surgeons. As soon as funds permitted, we paid a secretary for part-time work, which relieved me. When Miss Falconer resigned she was succeeded by Miss Smith, who remained for a short time. Mr. D. W. Karn of Karn Organ fame became President of the Board. His business often took him to Toronto and he made enquiries there, and through his influence we got Miss Sharpe, who had been night superintendent of the Toronto General Hospital. She was simply ideal in every respect. She knew her work thoroughly, was beloved by her nurses and patients, absolutely trusted by the Board, and by her bright courtesy made the hospital popular with the citizens generally. Under her, enlargement became necessary, and a wing had to be built. Mr. J. D. Patterson told the Board that, if they permitted, he would take the whole top floor of the new wing and equip it with the most up-to-date, modern surgical requirements. He visited hospitals in New York and Chicago, besides some Canadian hospitals, consulted the doctors and the manufacturers, and gave Woodstock the most completely equipped surgical department possible. We were all proud indeed of it. The curious tried to find how much it all cost, but fished in bad waters; for Mr. Patterson said, "The question is, does it meet our requirements here?" They could but reply, "Perfectly". "Well, that's what we want; the cost doesn't matter," was his invariable reply.

Nothing succeeds like success. The County Council financially helped the hospital. The Women's Auxiliary grew in numbers and usefulness, and the hospital became the most popular institution in the city — for Woodstock became a city.

The nurses had lived in the hospital, but it was not convenient in many ways, and their rooms were needed for strictly hospital purposes. With the generous help of Mr. J. D. Patterson and the enthusiasm of the Women's Auxiliary, a Nurses' Home was built next to the hospital. It is a very fine and beautiful building. They insisted on Mrs. Farthing and me coming from Montreal for the opening. They presented me with a gold key. Mr. E. W. Nesbitt, M.P., was President of the Board when it was opened. A group was standing around after the ceremony, and the gold key was being examined, when someone asked, "Will the key open the door?" Mrs. Sinclair, wife of Dr. Sinclair, a very intimate friend throughout my life in Woodstock, exclaimed, "Oh dear, no; do you think we would give him a key that would open the door?" Whereat there was much laughter!

On the preceding two pages — As Woodstock grew, so did the General Hospital. To the right may be seen Patterson House and behind it, Gissing House, both nurses' residences. On the left can be seen the West Wing which was added in 1927. As one passes our Hospital today, many more additions will be evident.

It was a great joy for my wife and me to see the consummation of our hopes for Woodstock, which had as finely equipped a hospital as any in the country. It was a glorious evolution.

When I left Woodstock they made me a life member of their Board of Governors which honour I greatly value.

Let me conclude this account of the hospital with a human story. I was President of the Hospital Board at the time and was looking for a janitor. A parishioner of mine, who was a fine character and who had a devoted wife, and children, had one weakness — he at times went off on terrible drinking sprees. On one occasion when he was on a spree, I found him in the bar of our worst-run hotel. I urged him to come home with me. He got quarrelsome and noisy, and when I got him outside, he squared up and wanted to fight me! However, I got him home. When the spree was over, he came to see me and said he heard that the hospital wanted a janitor, and he wanted me to appoint him. I said, "Dan, you would make a good janitor were it not for those sprees. What would these nurses do if you came back there in a drunken condition?" He said, "I give you my word of honour that while there I will not touch a drop. I feel the craving some time before I drink, and if I feel it coming on I will come and tell you beforehand. Give me a chance please!" I went up and talked it over with Miss Sharpe. I told her that I had great regard for him and I felt he would do as he promised. She said, "Bring him along; we'll try to help him." He was appointed. Miss Sharpe was most kind and he became devoted to her; and she had implicit confidence in him. He was an ideal janitor in every way, ever keen to serve Miss Sharpe and the hospital. In a short time we secured a house just opposite the hospital, and moved his family into it. He became "a part of the concern" — a small boy phrased it in another case. Everyone trusted, admired and respected Dan McKinnon. He idolized Miss Sharpe, who had really brought out the finest qualities which I was sure were in him. He was so happy in his work, nothing was a trouble to him. Miss Sharpe was God's instrument to make his life of real value to the Woodstock Hospital and the people which it served.

THE STORY OF THE BALLAD OF J. R. BIRCHALL

On a slushy day in February, two men were tramping, single file, through a swamp near Princeton, Ontario. Occasionally hunters might range through the swamp, for game was plentiful, and sometimes wood-cutters made their way in, but the sounds that rang out in the swamp that day were neither woodsman's axe nor hunter's gun. They were revolver shots fired by Birchall, at close range, instantly killing his victim, F. C. Benwell.

Birchall carefully removed from Benwell's clothing every possible mark of identification, left the body lying in the desolate waste ever since known as Benwell Swamp, and walked back to the Eastwood Station, taking the afternoon train to Niagara.

Four days later two young men, brothers, named Elvidge, went into the swamp to cut wood. A log too big to be moved had to be sawn in halves and preparing to do this, one of the men stepped over the log and planted his foot upon the frozen corpse. The body was removed to the Swarts undertaking parlors in the village of Princeton, and it was there the discovery was made that the man had been murdered. Two bullets had entered the back of his head, crossing within, in an almost perfect X.

At the inquest no identification was possible. When the body of the unknown young man, without mourners, was on its way to the cemetery the Anglican clergyman from Woodstock, who also officiated at St. Paul's in Princeton, met the hearse. He stopped — these were horse and buggy days — the situation was explained to him, he turned and preceded the little company to the grave, and read the burial service there.

That, however, was by no means the end of the story. A few days later the Elvidges returned to their work in the swamp, and there a few feet from where they had come upon the body they saw a cigar case marked "F. C. Benwell".

F. C. Benwell and another young man, named Pelly, had been brought by Birchall from England. They were to be taught farming, for an ample fee, on his wonderfully equipped non-existent farm in Ontario.

The newspapers, of course, carried the story, including the finding of F. C. Benwell's cigar case. Birchall and Pelly were still at Niagara, awaiting the return of Benwell, whom Mrs. Birchall and Pelly both believed to be visiting friends in Woodstock. Birchall had thus accounted for Benwell's absence. Now, he came up to Princeton to see if it had really been his young friend to whom this terrible thing had happened.

The village seethed with excitement. Summers Benham, a Princeton resident who remembered clearly the whole dreadful happenings, said "Princeton Cemetery had a crowd like Drumbo Fair when Benwell's body was exhumed".

Birchall stood by the open grave and identified the body as that of "poor Freddie". A well-known citizen of that time, in his usual state of exhilaration, leaned across the grave, pointed an accusing finger at Birchall and loudly proclaimed, "There's the devil that done it". Birchall gave his accuser a contemptuous stare, and the excited old fellow was hustled out of the cemetery.

On Page 110 — The Old Court House as it was in 1865. To the left can be seen the Old Registry Office and the Jail is in the background. Birchall's trial had to be held in the Town Hall because the present Court House was under construction, this old building having already been razed.

On Page 111 — The last trial held in the Old Court House. The prisoner in the dock in the foreground is unidentified.

This page — The "New" Registry Office entrance (the building has since been replaced) as it appeared to artist G. E. Payne in 1937. This building still stands on Hunter St. at the corner of Graham St.

On Page 113 — The trial of John Birchall in the Town Hall. Birchall can be seen in the dock, standing, facing the Judge, flanked by three bailiffs armed with staves. Many sketches were made at the trial by newspaper artists but this is the first known actual photograph of the trial to ever be published.

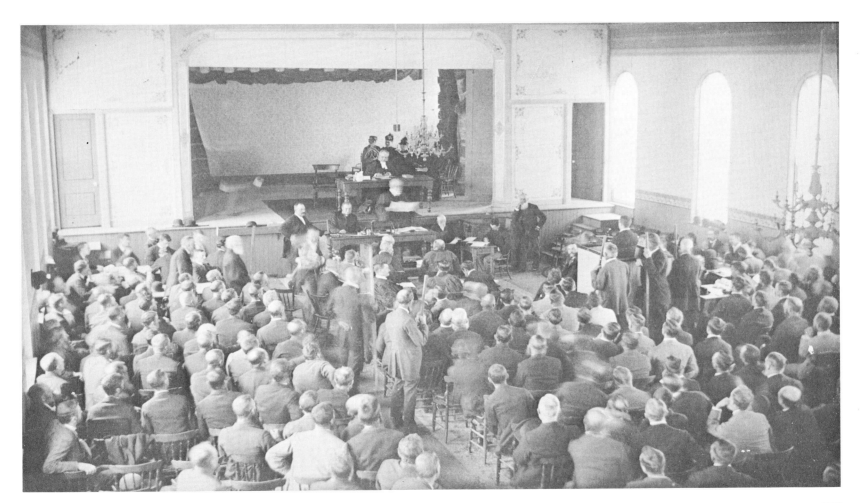

A few years previously Birchall and his wife had lent brilliance to Woodstock society by spending a season there as "Lord and Lady Somerset". They had returned to England somewhat hastily, to the regret of their acquaintances and the leading Woodstock merchants, but they had become well-known in the district during their stay. This made it possible for many people to identify Birchall. The conductor on the train, people at Eastwood station, had seen him come to Eastwood with young Benwell and leave without him. He had been seen in the vicinity of the swamp. All this, and other evidence piled up against him, he was convicted of the murder of Benwell, and hanged in the yard of Woodstock jail, November 14, 1890. The Birchall Ballad commemorates the crime, and Benwell's name is perpetuated in the Benwell Swamp, and on his grave in Princeton cemetery which bears this inscription:

In loving memory of
Frederick Cornwallis Benwell
Born 13th Sept. 1865
Murdered in the Township of Blenheim, Feb. 17, 1890.
Eldest son of Lt.-Col. Benwell of Cheltenham, England.
Formerly Captain 100th Regiment.

"What I do thou knowest not now, but thou shalt know hereafter."

On facing page — The Old Woodstock City Band as it appeared at the turn of the century.

114

THE BALLAD OF J. R. BIRCHALL

Come, all you tender Christians, wherever you may be,
    I pray you pay attention to these few words from me;
On the fourteenth of November, I am condemned to die
    For the murder of F. C. Benwell — upon a scaffold high.

My name is J. R. Birchall — that name I'll not deny,
    I leave my aged parents, in sorrow for to die;
For little did they think that in my youth and bloom
    I'd be taken to the scaffold to meet an awful doom.

Now Benwell was an Englishman, who had not yet a wife,
    He came out here to Canada to seek an honest life.
They said that I betrayed him unto a certain spot,
    And there with a revolver poor Benwell, he was shot.

I tried to play off innocent, but found it would not do;
    The evidence being against me, it proved I had no show.
The Judge he gave the sentence, the clerk he wrote it down,
    And to the scaffold I must go to meet my fearful doom.

My friends they came to see me, to take their last farewell;
    They seemed most broken-hearted to see me in my cell —
Saying, "Comrades, darling comrades, why shed those tears for me,
    For before tomorrow's sun shall set, from troubles I'll be free".

My wife she came to see me to take her last farewell,
    She said it was heart-rending to leave me in my cell.
She said, "My dearest husband, you know that you must die
    For the murder of F. C. Benwell, upon a scaffold high."

It was nine o'clock in the morning; I knew my doom was near;
    I bid farewell to all on earth, to friends and loved ones dear.
The last few words were spoken, the words "Thy will be done".
    The trap-door was now opened, and Birchall, he was hung.

On these pages are photos of Woodstock taken in 1897 from the steeple of Old Knox Church on Brock St. by Sid Coppins. If placed end to end they would show a panoramic view of the Town as it appeared at that time. From the lower left and running clockwise, the views are as follows: 1) Looking south towards the Grand Trunk Railway, McIntosh's pond and Bower Hill; 2) Looking west, Broadway School is seen on the left and Canada Furniture Manufacturers in the background; 3) Looking northwest, Dundas St. Methodist Church, Old Chalmers Church and the Opera House (now the Capitol Theatre) tower can be seen; 4) Here, looking north, can be seen the "new" Fire Hall, Central School tower (long since removed), the Court House, Knox Church, and at the end of Perry St., Poole's Grocery; 5) Looking northeast, Central and New St. Paul's Churches are plainly visible as is the tower on the Town Hall. The "new" Market building can be seen but the Dundas St. Post Office building cannot, having been built several years later; 6) Looking east southeast, few present day landmarks are visible. On the extreme right is the Rapson baseball park, in the centre can be seen the Grand Trunk water tower, and in the right background, Woodstock College; 7) Looking south southeast towards what is now Southside Park, the Grant Tannery and Water Works buildings can be seen. Finkle St. runs south, up the hill.

On Page 118 — The Concrete Pipe Works on Riddell St. about 1900. As can be seen, horsepower and manpower were put to full use. On Page 119 — The interior of McHardy's Meat Market just after the turn of the century. The late Ernest Sibley is the gentleman on the right. On this page — Left — Woodstock, from its beginning, was noted for its hotels. In the 1850's, there were eighteen hotels in Town at the same time, Here are two that have withstood the passing of time (even to the present day) as they appeared about 1905. Notice the taxi in front of Hotel Oxford. Above — A Circus today draws a crowd just as it did in 1910 at the Fairgrounds. On Page 121 — For ages, man has relied on the horse for power. Here are four views of "Dobbin" at work in Woodstock early in this century. Upper left shows construction in progress at what is now Ralston Purina Co. Ltd.; upper right was taken in a gravel pit within the city limits; lower right shows a familiar sight in early days, the town junk dealer; lower right is the long forgotten "honey wagon", a vehicle which went out of use with the end of "privies" 'in the City. These photos and that of the Oxford Hotel were printed from the original glass negatives.

FIRE

Woodstock was inaugurated as a city in 1901 but her fire department had been of city calibre several years prior to this.

To obtain this status was a long uphill grind for all those interested in fire protection. The battle for a fire hall started in 1880 but every bylaw was doomed even before the ink was dry. In 1899 the clouds of dissension cleared and under the leadership of W. A. Karn, who was chairman of the fire and light committee, a plan was presented to the people which they accepted wholeheartedly and the new hall was erected the same year. The cost of building and installing the latest in electric alarm systems was $10,000. The architect was J. E. Tisdale of Woodstock.

Horse-drawn equipment was still being used when the hall was opened. "Farmer", the faithful fire horse, was completing 15 years in the service of Woodstock. He was assisted by three others and their new stables were located on the ground floor and the firemen had the second floor. The bell in the tower was rather unique as it had the names of the council engraved on it.

The brigade consisted of 15 men, five of whom spent the night at the hall. Three were on duty at all times. They were Chief Johnston, who had been made chief in 1873, driver McLean with 15 years service and Alf Thurlow with 12 years of service.

The feature attraction of the hall was to see the firemen slide down the pole from their quarters as they went through their daily practice runs.

Woodstock was rather fortunate, thanks to the efficiency of the brigade, that no fire got out of hand although the LaFrance fire was considered a serious fire, but it was able to be contained in its immediate area.

"Farmer" stayed on until 1903 when he was retired on January 17, 1903, but it was not until September 1920 that the last of this type of equipment was replaced. The council had decided to motorize the brigade on March 26, 1920, but it was September 10 when the equipment arrived.

Since that time the department has continued to grow as the city required it and today it consists of Fire Chief Gordon Tripp and 35 full-time firefighters. The equipment housed at the station consists of one 1929 pumper which will pump 600 gallons p.m., one 1952 pumper capable of 600 gallons p.m., one 1956 pumper capable of 840 g.p.m., one 1957 portable pump capable of 200 g.p.m., one 1939 aerial and ladder truck carrying a 65-ft. aerial ladder and 210 feet of hand ladders and one 1960 station wagon.

Woodstock's Fire Horses in action on Dundas St.

Within the city are to be found 417 hydrants with 23,603 feet of water main of 6-inch or over, and over 8,914 feet of water main under 6-inch, making 67.5 miles in all. There are three reservoirs holding a total of 2,400,000 gallons of water, and the department carries 6,000 feet of 2½" hose and 1,800 feet of 1½" hose.

In comparing the cost we find no record prior to 1908 but that year the cost of operating with horse-drawn equipment and a seven-man crew (permanent) was $5,700.00, while in 1966 the cost with a 35-man crew and completely motorized equipment cost $263,738.72.

PEOPLE

One seldom becomes famous in his own home town, in fact, famous people are often unknown in their own town until after they do become famous and then everybody recognizes them. From Woodstock, many have gone out and made a name for themselves while others have gained a place through notoriety.

Several women are among former Woodstock residents who have attained fame in their own specialized field. These include Florence Carlyle, the artist, Evelyn Fletcher, a musician, Margaret Beattie, who married Timothy Eaton and assisted him in creating his mercantile empire, and the notorious Cassie Chadwick.

Men of Woodstock have also achieved fame in entirely different fields. Such were Rev. Geo. McKay, the "Black Bearded Barbarian" who took the gospel to Formosa, and the fabulous Jo Boyle who made and lost fortunes overnight but persevered in the Yukon and in Russia until even the Russians declare, "Brother, there's a man". Thos. L. "Carbide" Wilson chose the field of science and perfected calcium carbide. He is one of the few who returned to his home and gifted the city with a memorial. In the field of politics many who served Oxford have gone on to greater achievements, such as Sir

Francis Hinks, Pattullo, Carroll, to name a few. Sports have produced many great teams but the outstanding individual has been "Bob" Hayward, the Oxford chicken farmer who plucked the Harmsworth Trophy from the U.S.A.

Miss Florence Carlyle, the artist, was not born here but came to Woodstock at an early age. Her father was the local school inspector. At an early age she showed unusual ability with oils and her mother encouraged her. Her studio was located at 332 Simcoe St. In 1890 she went to Paris, returning to Canada in 1896. The Royal Canadian Academy elected her as the first woman associate in 1897. In 1899 she opened a studio in New York but spent most of her time in Europe. Her best known works were done in Crowborough, Sussex, England, where she moved in 1913. The works of Miss Carlyle are to be seen hanging in the Royal Academy in London, England, the National Art Gallery at Ottawa and at leading galleries throughout Canada, U.S.A. and Europe. Several of her paintings are to be found here in Woodstock.

Miss Evelyn Fletcher was born in Woodstock, the daughter of Ashton Fletcher, Q.C. She spent her childhood here and completed her schooling by attending schools in England, France and Germany. She accepted a position of teacher of music at the Hamilton Ladies' College and later at Bishop Strachan School at Toronto.

While teaching here she developed the "Fletcher Musical Kindergarten System" and patented it in 1897 while still in her early twenties. This system revolutionized the teaching of music to children. She was called to Europe where she lectured before the Incorporate Society of Music, the Royal Normal College in England, also at Brussels, Berlin, Leipzig and Paris.

About the system: it recognizes the nature of childish minds, its powers, its needs and its possibilities. It leads from nursery rhymes and songs to the handling of new toys cut out of wood, whose names are soon learned by songs and stories — about Mrs. Treble Clef, Mrs. Bass Clef, Mrs. Whole Note and her family of notes. This fulfils one of the first of Fobel's principles — acquiring knowledge through contact.

Two local characters who added a great deal of interest to Woodstock seventy years ago. On the left is Timmy "Irish for mine" Cahill. Above is "Negro Rance", a handyman who, at the time of Birchall's imprisonment, acted as his valet.

Margaret Beattie Eaton, who at the age of twenty-one married Timothy Eaton, was raised east of Woodstock of Irish parentage. From her humble beginning in St. Marys she made her way about the feminine departments in their store and through her introduction of mirrors in the millinery department developed a department which is still the leading one in their chain of stores operating under the Eaton name. She did not neglect clerks in her husband's store who were ill and she would pay them a visit and take along some small article to cheer them. She was considered by the clerks as the founder of Eaton's Employee Welfare Group, an idea that has been copied by many. Throughout her lifetime she was a guiding influence in this mercantile empire.

On the other side of the picture we have the notorious Cassie Chadwick. Born at Eastwood, she dreamed of a life of splendor and set out to achieve it.

Through careful planning she was able to swindle local farmers and merchants but when she presented a bogus note she was apprehended and brought to trial at Woodstock. She was released and her parents immediately sent her to Cleveland to live with her sister.

Here she started all over again by borrowing money on her sister's furniture and moved into high society. She met and married a prominent doctor and when her picture appeared in the local press she was recognized by the money lenders who immediately presented their demands for full payment. Her husband had the wedding annulled and she was sent to prison. Upon her release she started all over again with similar results.

Finally she returned to Cleveland and pulled the biggest swindle ever master-minded by a woman. She again married a doctor and as Mrs. Chadwick began to move in the circle that had so bluntly excluded her on her first venture into crime in the U.S.A.

Top — "Seven Gables", the home of Judge McQueen long after it had seen its heyday. Bottom — "The Firs", home of Jo Boyle which still stands on Dundas St. opposite the statue of Springbank Snow Countess.

Among these people she made it known that she was interested in starting a banking firm and wanted others to join her. Eventually she persuaded several leading citizens to go to New York with her, claiming that she would secure funds from her benefactor, Andrew Carnegie. She claimed to be his illegitimate daughter. By a well-planned ruse she gained admission to the Carnegie house and returned with a large package supposedly containing securities. Fortunately her would-be partners backed out leaving her to play her trump hand alone.

She deposited her securities as collateral for a small short term loan in a Cleveland suburb bank but upon arrival home called the bank and asked for a duplicate copy of the list of securities she had left with the manager. The bank obliged and now she had a list of her supposedly good securities listed on bank stationery complete with the manager's signature. With this type of collateral she commenced her greatest swindle.

She was a small stooped-over woman and not too attractive, so in order to gain attention she always invited young attractive debutantes to accompany her and would favour them with such gifts as pianos or exclusive clothes or jewellery. Her plan was kept operating by her borrowing off one place to pay another until her credit was established and if she was slow in paying they hesitated to ask her in fear of losing her patronage.

The bubble burst when a note in Boston became due and she ignored it. It was placed in court and before long others appeared. Cassie had gone too far and could not redeem herself. The package of supposedly good securities was opened and found to be worthless. The banker committed suicide and she was returned to prison. Here she died and was returned to Woodstock for burial in the Anglican Cemetery. Her funeral was the first item from Woodstock taken by newsreel cameramen for presentation at local movie houses.

Perhaps the most outstanding man to leave the Woodstock area was Rev. Leslie McKay of East Zorra. He entered the ministry of the Presbyterian Church and requested permission to go to China as a missionary. As Canada was not sending missionaries out, it was arranged for him to go under the Mission Board of Great Britain.

His arrival in China was not welcomed and his meetings were continually being stoned and broken up but he continued and "The Black Bearded Barbarian" began to gain followers. From this humble beginning he devoted his life to the Orient and was soon accepted by the people in general including many of the warlike tribes living in the mountains. His outstanding achievement was the establishing of Oxford College on Formosa which today is considered as one of the highest seats of learning in the East.

The name Jo Boyle is almost a legend in itself. Jo received his last years of schooling at Woodstock College but left to go to sea. While travelling to all parts of the world he developed a mannerism that made him a leader. His final voyage as a sailor was climaxed with a mutiny which the captain claimed Jo suppressed single-handed.

Returning to shore life, he became interested in race horses and boxers. After a few good years he landed in California with a has-been boxer and no money. Here he learned of the gold strike in the Yukon and joined in the rush. After a death-defying trip into the Yukon, Boyle succeeded in staking a strike. He claimed that if most of the gold was found in the creeks then the proper thing to do was to get equipment that could dredge the beds and secure all the gold. He sold others on the idea and before long dredges were brought in overland and Boyle made another fortune.

Then came the War of 1914-18. Boyle formed a battalion of machine gunners at his own expense and brought them east and on to Europe. In Europe they were disbanded as replacement troops and he was without a job. About this time Russia was asking for help to untangle her railways. As Boyle was not too popular due to his desire to get busy again he was asked to go. He was happy once more and in a short time the officer with the solid gold pips on his shoulder had the railways humming again. Then came the revolution.

On Page 126 — The home of Robert Campbell at 195 Vansittart Ave. in 1890. Note the lightning arrestors. On Page 127 — This stately home at 312 Light St. was the residence of Craig McKay, K.C. Both these homes have been renovated many times since these photos were taken. On Page 129 — Two notes which prove the faith Woodstonians had in Jo Boyle. In 1916, Mr. H. McIntosh loaned Jo almost $3,000 to finance one of his ventures.

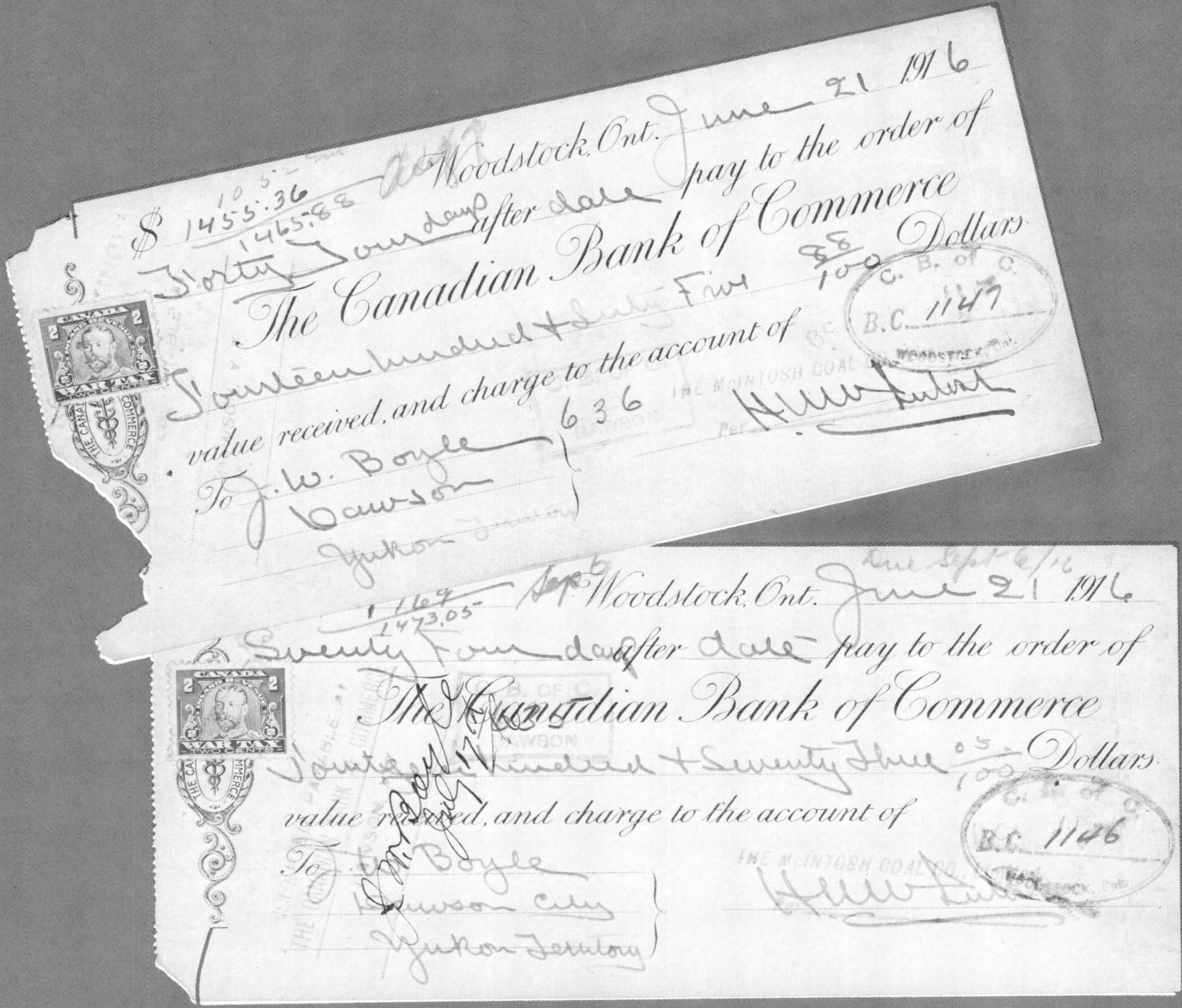

Cheque 1:

$ 1455.36
1465.88

Woodstock, Ont. June 21 1916

Forty Four days after date pay to the order of

The Canadian Bank of Commerce

Fourteen hundred & Sixty Five 88/100 Dollars

value received, and charge to the account of

636

To J. W. Boyle
Dawson
Yukon Territory

B.C. 1147

Per ___

Cheque 2:

Due Sept 6/16

1464
1473.05

Woodstock, Ont. June 21 1916

Seventy Four days after date pay to the order of

The Canadian Bank of Commerce

Fourteen hundred & Seventy Three 05/100 Dollars

value received, and charge to the account of

To J. W. Boyle
Dawson City
Yukon Territory

B.C. 1146

Under the disguise of Red Cross officials he led a party into the building where the Crown Jewels of Roumania were stored and removed them just before the members of the revolution came for the same purpose. He managed to successfully drive a train through both the German and Russian lines and make good his escape into Roumania and return the jewels to the Queen. He remained there and assisted in developing the famous oil fields of that country. While in the oil fields he suffered a stroke and it is reported that the Queen herself nursed him back to health. He remained there and upon his death was returned to London, England, for burial.

"Carbide" Wilson, the discoverer of acetylene gas, was born at Princeton, Ontario, and today the steel industry is able to create wonders through the use of acetylene in the field of welding. Thos. L. Wilson was also active in the development of carbide gas which is still considered as the sailor's saviour. It is used to light buoys and markers in the channels of the great waterways as an aid to navigation.

His gift to Woodstock, the Wilson home on Vansittart Avenue, is one of the finest homes in Woodstock. The St. Joseph Convent now occupies the building. One of the outstanding features of the house is the leaded windows portraying famous paintings. The property was recently declared an historic site and is marked with a plaque.

In the field of politics there are many, some of the outstanding ones being Sir Francis Hinks, the leader of the Reform Party who was active in raising funds to establish the Great Western Railroad. He was later knighted and made governor of the Windward Islands.

George Brown, the Liberal leader who became publisher of the Globe and Mail, was an active campaigner in Oxford. His influence among the Zorras is still felt as only in recent elections have Conservative candidates secured a majority of votes.

Gus Pattullo, a member of a prominent local family, went to British Columbia to become premier of that province.

Hon. D. M. Sutherland, a member of the Conservative party, was the Minister of National Defence in the R. B. Bennett Government during the depression years of the 1930's. He still makes his home in Embro and with opening of a second senior public school in Woodstock he was honoured by having it named after him. A doctor by profession as well as a soldier, he was wounded in France and returned to Canada to raise a battalion and return with them as their Colonel.

Robert Hayward, the chicken farmer, was born and raised at Embro. Always interested in racing and boats, he accepted a position on the team of Miss Supertest II and became the driver of Miss Supertest III when she defeated the best in American drivers to pluck the famous Harmsworth Trophy from their grasp. On September 10, 1961, he was killed trying to avoid a crash while driving Miss Supertest II at Detroit.

On facing page — The east side of Vansittart Ave. between Dundas and Hunter Sts. during the 1890's. This was the Peers terrace, most of which is still standing today.

STREET NAMES OF WOODSTOCK

I love old things
Streets of old cities
Crowded with ghosts.
— Wilson McDonald.

To many residents of Woodstock the street names have little significance. To the older generation they breathe history, British history, Canadian history and local history.

It is interesting to know how and why these names were given. In some cases it was quite easy to trace their origin, in other cases more difficult.

Woodstock proper, that is to say the government appropriation for the site of the town, embraced that portion of lands lying north of Dundas Street and west of Riddell Street, bounded by the Thames River and the second concession of Blandford. This original town plot was founded by Governor Simcoe in 1795.

Dundas Street was undoubtedly the first street named and was so-called by Simcoe after Henry Dundas, Viscount Melville, Secretary of State. This road, the Governor's Road, was cut through the bush and intended to be a highway to London, which town Simcoe thought had all the qualifications for the capital of Upper Canada. Owing to the difficulty of transportation he was forced to relinquish this plan.

In 1931 a cairn was erected at Dundas by the Historic Sites and Monuments Committee bearing the following inscription:

Dundas Street
The Governor's Road.

Planned by Lieutenant-Governor Simcoe in 1793 as a military road and commercial highway between Lake Ontario and the River Thames to promote settlement of the province. Laid out and constructed by the Queen's Rangers under his orders and named in honor of Hon. Henry Dundas, Secretary of State for War and the Colonies.

Woodstock was a distinctive English settlement. The early citizens were cultured men of influence and wealth and many were connected, in some way, with the British Army or Navy. In the years following the Napoleonic Wars many officers resigned their commissions and emigrated to Canada. Not a few of these military men congregated in this neighborhood either for the sake of congenial friendship or because they were attracted by the natural beauty of the surrounding country. They erected stately homes, most of them large square houses built of white brick and built with many extensions such as gun rooms, coach houses and a few boasted of ballrooms.

One of the first of these English men to arrive was Captain Andrew Drew. He had entered the British Navy in 1806 and served through the last stages of the Napoleonic Wars. In 1832 he was sent out to Canada by Rear Admiral Henry VanSittart to locate and report on lands purchased by VanSittart who wished to establish his sons in this new country. In the Rebellion of 1837 Captain Drew was senior naval officer in the colony. Rev. William Bettridge, once an officer in the regular service, gathered together for consultation such men as Col. A. W. Light, Major Buller, Captain Graham, Admiral VanSittart and Captain Drew. It was decided to place at the command of Sir Alan McNab such a contingent as might be required. A United States steamer "The Caroline" was employed carrying supplies and munitions of war from Buffalo for the provisional government of which McKenzie was the head. The character of the situation was presented to Scott, then in command of the United States forces, but his sympathies were with the enemies of Canada. Heroic measures were then decided on and Captain Drew was given a free hand. This officer selected his men for the hazardous task of cutting out and destroying the Caroline. Several Woodstock men were among those chosen. It is said that Col. Light was the last man to pass down the side of the doomed craft as she swung head foremost toward the Falls. In 1840 Captain Drew was forced to leave Canada because of several attempts on his life.

On facing page — Map of the Town of Woodstock, 1855.

Map
OF THE TOWN OF
WOODSTOCK
Canada West

Then too, Captain Drew gave the land on which St. Paul's Church was erected. For some years Captain Drew lived on the corner of Rathbourne Avenue and Sydenham Street and this house has always been known as the Drew Homestead. It was built by Nelson Bendish, a nephew of the famous Lord Nelson. So Drew Street, when you know a little of the history of the gallant officer, Captain A. Drew, stands out as an important street, and Nelson Street is not merely a reminder of the triumph over the French at the Battle of the Nile, for it was named after a descendant of the Nelson family.

Although the western portion of the city was first set aside for the town, the nucleus of a village grew around St. Paul's Church and grew rapidly, while all else remained a wilderness.

Money contributed and collected by Vice-Admiral Henry Van-Sittart was sent out to Canada for the erection of a church and the living was offered to Rev. William Bettridge with the pledge of one hundred pounds a year and one hundred acres of cleared land. Bettridge began life in the British Army and during the Peninsular Wars was an aide-de-camp to the Duke of Wellington. He was present at the celebrated ball given by the Duchess of Richmond in Brussels before the Battle of Waterloo. It is said that Bettridge met his wife, Mary Hounsfield, in Paris when the Allied armies were there. Abandoning his military career, he took his degree at Cambridge University and was ordained in 1824. In 1834 he took charge of St. Paul's Church. The name of this dignified and eloquent rector is not found among our street names, yet Lawrason and Hounsfield can be traced back to this family. Mrs. Belle Lawrason was a daughter of Canon Bettridge, and Mary Hounsfield was the maiden name of his wife.

The last interment in St. Paul's cemetery was that of Canon Bettridge in 1879.

Beale Street derives its name from Major E. Beale, who held a commission in the Second Oxford Regiment. He received the appointment of Major on April 23, 1838.

Darius E. Riddle was a brother-in-law of Admiral VanSittart but the street that bears his name has been converted into Riddell.

East of Riddell Street we find an Edward, a Mary, a Grace and a George Street. These streets are named after the children of Thos. J. Cottle, an early resident who lived at Altadore.

It is interesting to know that a horticultural society was formed in Woodstock on April 2, 1852, and its first exhibition was held at Altadore. An orange tree and an aloe tree that were shown by Mrs. East, Admiral VanSittart's sister, attracted great attention. Then too it was at Altadore that the Prince of Wales, afterwards Edward VII, was entertained in 1860. The Cottle family came from the West Indies.

Another man who played no small part in the early history of the town was Captain Phillip Graham. In 1837 he was the treasurer of a committee authorized to raise 3,000 pounds for the erection of a court house. The building stood on the site of the present court house and was torn down and the present beautiful building erected on the original site.

Light Street owes its name to Col. Alexander Whalley Light of the Royal Engineers. Light resided at Lytes Carie, about three miles west of the town. Col. Light's name was honorably mentioned in the Rebellion of 1837. He was one of the first men to suggest the building of the Great North Western Railway which was opened in 1853.

Col. R. A. Hunter took a keen interest in the educational problems of the growing town and was instrumental in having a grammar school erected in 1848. This school was built at the corner of Graham and Hunter Streets. The following advertisement for this school appeared in the Sentinel-Review of September 20, 1867:

"Classes for instruction in book-keeping, mensuration, drawing and mapping will be opened next week under the superintendence of Mr. Byrne, the assistant master, also trigonometry and surveying. Mr. B.——— has had two years' experience as a teacher of drawing and mathematics; also ten years' training under R. A. Gray, Esq., Civil Engineer and Surveyor for the County of Dublin. George Strachan, Head Master".

On facing page — Map of the Town of Woodstock, 1874.

PLAN OF THE
TOWN OF
WOODSTOCK

Scale 10 Ch.s 1 inch

Buller Street perpetuates the name of Major Edward Buller, an officer in the 3rd Oxford Regiment whose name was mentioned along with that of Drew and Light in the Rebellion of '37.

Since 1886 there has been an Ingersoll Avenue, which carries the name of Colonel Ingersoll, second Registrar of Oxford County. Previous to that year the street extending east from the River Thames to VanSittart Street was known as Barwick Street, no doubt named after Major Hugh Barwick, County Treasurer, who came to Woodstock in 1834, and the continuation of this street from VanSittart Street to Riddell Street is known as St. Marys Street.

It would be difficult to find a more beautiful street than VanSittart Avenue, with its lovely homes, well kept lawns, wide boulevards and the double row of stately maples. It is indeed a fitting memorial to Vice Admiral Henry VanSittart who has always and will always be known as the man who made Woodstock. Henry VanSittart was born at Bisham Abbey, Berkshire, in 1779. He entered the British Navy as midshipman in 1791 and served through the Revolutionary and Napoleonic Wars. In 1830 he was promoted to Rear Admiral and in 1841 to Vice Admiral.

The VanSittart family came out to Canada in 1834. The trip to Woodstock was sadly interrupted, for the wife of the Admiral became seriously ill and passed away at Saratoga on July 2, 1834. Mr. William Grey claimed the honor of moving this family here during that summer. Sleds drawn by two yoke of oxen were used in making the trip through the practically unbroken roads from Niagara Falls. After the completion of the family tomb at St. Paul's the body of Mrs. VanSittart was brought here on December 5, 1834. Today that casket along with others of this outstanding family remains in a good state of preservation.

Anne Jameson's "Winter Studies and Summer Rambles in Canada", written in 1836 and 1837, describes Woodstock as "fast rising into an important town and says that the whole district, for its scenery, fertility and advantages of every kind, is perhaps the finest in Canada". The society in this neighborhood is particularly good, gentlemen of family, superior education and large capital. Admiral VanSittart has already expended upwards of twenty thousand pounds in purchases and improvements. His house is a real curiosity. It is two or three miles from the highroad in the midst of the forest and looks as if a number of log huts had jostled against each other and stuck there. I imagine he had begun by erecting a log house, then in need of space had added another, then another and so on, all different shapes and sizes and full of a seaman's contrivances, odd galleries, passages, porticos, corridors, saloons, cabins and cupboards. If the outside reminded one of an African village, the interior was no less like that of a man of war. The drawing room which occupies an entire building is really a noble room with a chimney in which they pile twenty logs at once. Around this room a gallery, well lighted with windows from without, through which there is a constant circulation of air, keeping the room warm in winter and cool in summer. The Admiral has besides so many ingenious and inexplicable contrivances for warming and airing his house that no insurance office will insure him on any terms. Altogether it was the most strangely picturesque building I ever beheld. The Admiral's sister, an accomplished woman of independent fortune, has lately arrived from Europe to take up her residence in the wilds.

On Sunday we attended the pretty little church at Woodstock which was filled by the neighboring settlers of all classes. The service was well read and the hymns sung by the ladies of the congregations.

By the naming of Admiral Street and Vansittart Avenue we have perpetuated the name of this noble family, not only in Woodstock but in Canada. For many years another street derived its name from this same source. The present Brant Street was formerly Henry Street.

The Right Honorable Nicholas VanSittart, Baron Bexley, son of Henry VanSittart, Governor of Bengal, was a cousin of Admiral VanSittart and thus we account for a Bexley Street.

In Niagara Falls there is a Delatre Street and perhaps we may draw on our imagination and think our Delatre Street was named after the same man.

Lower left — The Vansittart home. Upper left — The Drew "homestead" at the corner of Rathbourne Ave. and Sydenham St. Upper right — The Finkle home on Mill St. just south of Park Row. For many years this beautiful old home was used as the Children's Shelter. Right — Dr. R. A. Fyfe, first principal of the Canadian Literary Institute.

137

In 1831 the land given to the Harbour and Dock Company at Niagara Falls was surveyed and the streets named after the officials connected with the company. Colonel Delatre was the president of the company. From 1832 he lived at Lundy's Lane until a year previous to his sudden death on the steamer from Niagara to Toronto. His home, known as Delatre Lodge, was at the corner of Victoria and Front Streets. He is buried at Lundy's Lane. I have previously stated that Admiral VanSittart's wife died at Saratoga and I feel sure that this same Colonel Delatre, full of old world sympathy and hospitality, had been most kind to the bereaved family, so perhaps that is why the name of Delatre was suggested for one of our streets.

Oxford Street, like Oxford County, takes its name from Oxford, the capital of Oxfordshire, an inland county of England. The history of Oxford can be traced back to the time of Alfred the Great who established schools of literature there. The city arms show an ox crossing a ford.

Winnett Street was opened in 1844 and was probably named after James Winnett, a colonel of the 4th Regiment Oxford Militia, whose appointment was made in 1838.

Yeo Street was in existence and was named in 1836. It may have been named after Sir James Yeo who served on Lake Ontario in the War of 1812.

The great general under whom these early citizens served was not forgotten, for we have a Duke as well as a Wellington Street.

The loyalty and love of these men to their mother land is most suitably expressed in the naming of certain other streets. Woodstock has a King Street, a Queen, a Princess, a Victoria and an Albert, an Adelaide and even a Kent Street. These all bespeak of Royalty.

York, afterwards Toronto, was named by Governor Simcoe in honor of Prince Frederick, Duke of York. Other settlements used this name and we have a York Street. Yet this street might derive its name from the Archbishop of York for there is every reason to believe that Canterbury Street here as well as in other Ontario cities was so called after the Archbishop of Canterbury who was the first Angli-can Archbishop to visit Canada.

The reign of Queen Victoria left its imprint, for there is a Melbourne Street; Lord Melbourne, you remember, was Victoria's first prime minister.

Russel Street is not as well known nor yet as important as Lord John Russel whose name it bears. It was Lord Russel who in 1839 introduced into the British Parliament a bill for the union of the Canadas. Upper and Lower Peel Street suggests Sir Robert Peel, who abolished the Corn Laws.

In looking over the city directory the names of several governor generals may be found, Simcoe, Sydenham, Metcalfe, Cathcart, Elgin and Dufferin.

Colonel John Graves Simcoe was governor in 1792, Lord Sydenham in 1838, and he was succeeded by Sir Chas. Metcalfe who arrived in Canada in 1843. After two years in office he resigned on account of ill health and was followed by Cathcart, a lieutenant general in the British Army. In 1847 Lord Elgin was appointed governor general.

Perhaps the most popular governor was Lord Dufferin. The streets bearing these names are scattered and the growth of the city can be traced by the date of the naming of these streets. This plan of perpetuating the names of the governor generals should not have been neglected and we should have a Lorne, a Lawnsdowne, a Stanley, Aberdeen, Minto, Grey, Connaught, Devonshire, Byng and a Willingdon.

Henry and John Finkle, father and uncle of Mr. H. J. Finkle, former postmaster, owned large grist mills on the present Mill Street. The name of Finkle will be kept fresh in our memories by these streets, Finkle and Mill.

In 1845 the first judge in this district was appointed, David Shank McQueen, and that fact is recorded by the naming of McQueen Street.

Broadway was for many years known as Bishop Street, probably after Henry Bishop, a contractor, who was a resident of Woodstock in 1836.

Brock Street recalls the War of 1812 for it was at Queenstown that General Sir Isaac Brock lost his life.

The home of the late Dr. Levi Perry has the distinction of being the oldest house in Woodstock. It was built in 1827 and is situated to the south of the street that bears his name.

Main seems rather an unimportant street, but in the early days it was one of the busy streets of the town. The south side of it was built up with warehouses and it was here that the grain was bought and shipped by rail. Woodstock had some reputation as a grain market in those days. One of the outstanding grain brokers was Thomas Phelan and we have a Phelan Street.

In 1856 Market Street was opened as an accommodation to the inhabitants that they might have easier access to the market.

Reeve Street was opened in 1854 that there might be a direct street from Dundas Street to the depot of the Great Western Railway.

Dover and Railway Streets are sad reminders of an enterprise, the building of the Port Dover Railway, that was a financial disaster to

Vansittart Avenue in 1901 looking south towards Buller St.

many prominent citizens years ago.

Wilson Street recalls the name of Mr. William Wilson, the father of J. L. Wilson. Mr. Wilson was a member of the first town council in 1851 and had the distinction of polling the greatest number of votes at that election. He was mayor in 1862 and 1863.

The trustees of the Literary Institute were desirous of extending their property northward across Walter Street as a bylaw was passed giving consent to open a street to the north but running parallel with Walter Street and the said street was called College Avenue.

Just why such an obscure street should be known as Fyfe Avenue is lamentable, but its proximity to the Canadian Literary Institute of which Rev. R. A. Fyfe was the first principal must have been the reason. This seat of learning, better known to most of us as the Baptist College, was opened in 1860 with an enrolment of 200 pupils, one-third of whom had the ministry in view.

Chapel and Burtch are significant names, for in 1836 a Baptist chapel was built on the corner of Dundas and Chapel Streets on land donated by Deacon Archibald Burtch. This chapel was sold to St. Paul's Church after the erection of the First Baptist Church on Adelaide Street and the building moved across the street. Later it was destroyed by fire.

Other prominent Baptist names are drawn to our attention by the discovery of a Teeple, a Hatch and a Pavey Street. Henry and Walter Streets are also named after the sons of Archibald Burtch.

Until 1868 Norwich Avenue was known as Oxford Street. A bylaw was passed in that year, changing the name to Norwich Avenue because the road led to Norwich, a village as old as Woodstock. The second post office in Oxford County was established in Norwich with Ingersoll claiming the first.

Cronyn Street was a part of the Clergy Reserves and bears the name of Bishop Cronyn of the London District.

An interesting bit of political news concerns Hincks Street. Sir Francis Hincks was the first representative of Oxford in 1840. At that election the polling booth was at the home of James Murray, a blacksmith. The polls were open from Monday until Saturday and 1165 votes were polled. The candidates were Sir Francis Hincks, editor of the Examiner, a sturdy Reform paper, and Peter Carrol, a surveyor of West Oxford. Hincks was elected by a majority of 31.

To the Peers family we owe the names of Anne, Maude and Young Streets, after the wife and daughter of the late John Peers. Young was the maiden name of his first wife.

Mr. George Laycock was the publisher of the Western Progress, a newspaper first published on November 14, 1851. Isabelle and Bee Streets derive their names from Isabelle and Beatrice, his two daughters.

The southwest corner of the city, known to us as the Gore, has an interesting history. In the years following the Crimean War, Woodstock enjoyed a real estate boom. This portion of the town was surveyed and named by Colonel A. W. Light and many of the streets are named after battles and generals of the war.

The Battle of Waterloo was one of the turning points in the world's history and we find a Waterloo Street, but Duke and Wellington are not near.

Raglan recalls the name of Fitzroy James Henry Raglan, an English Baron who was commander-in-chief with the rank of field marshal during the war. He fought at the Battle of Alma and there is an Alma Street.

General Canrobert was a famous French commander who also figured prominently at the Battle of Alma.

John Thomas Brundell Cardigan entered the British Army in 1824. Family influence and wealth procured for him rapid promotion and during the Crimean War he was appointed Brigadier in command of the Light Brigade. It was Cardigan who led the famous six hundred in the death charge at Bala Clava October 25th, 1854.

Sir George Cathcart was killed at the Battle of Inkerman, November 5th, 1854.

With a Waterloo, a Duke, a Wellington, a Raglan, an Alma, also a Canrobert, a Cardigan and a Cathcart street, we have in these street names a short story of the Crimean War.

Our streets are historical in name and may the custom of numbering them never become the custom in our city. We would not care to be robbed of the romance of pioneer days.

Above — Teenagers played many more lawn sports sixty years ago than they do today. Here is a game of bowls being enjoyed on the lawn at 312 Light St.

On facing page—This book would not be complete without this beautiful old picture of our Court House, draped in mourning for King Edward VII in May, 1910.

THE WOODSTOCK, THAMES VALLEY AND INGERSOLL ELECTRIC RAILWAY

The use of electricity in Woodstock dates back to the '80s when electricity was generated at the corner of Mill and Main Streets. This supplied power to a limited number of business establishments in the uptown area. This factor was mentioned freely in any publicity given the town, with the result that Dr. S. Ritter Ickes and J. Armstrong, two influential gentlemen promoting the electric railways in south-western Ontario, arrived in town in 1897. Their ambition was to form a street railway company in Woodstock. After a careful study of the situation they realized that it would not be economical to try and operate strictly within the town. They then decided to attempt to create a suburban line operating between Woodstock and Ingersoll via Beachville.

Once the necessary groundwork was completed they retained the legal firm of Wallace and Little and began negotiating for a 99-year franchise. The lights in the town council chamber burned late as the town fathers considered the question from all angles. The result was that they offered the Woodstock, Thames Valley and Ingersoll Electric Street Railway a franchise for fifty years. Many of the councillors had preferred a twenty-five year franchise.

On facing page — the now famous "Estelle" on her maiden run in 1900 flanked by proud dignitaries representing Woodstock, Ingersoll and the Railway Company. This page — These photos of Dundas Street in 1905 show its appearance shortly after the "Estelle" and "The City of Woodstock" began their runs.

The sale of stock began immediately and by January, 1900, the sum of $100,000.00 had been raised locally. The promoters added $13,000 to this, giving them sufficient capital. Once the necessary capital was raised the council immediately made way for construction to begin by preparing the necessary by-laws. The by-law was passed on January 23, and it stipulated that the work would have to be completed within 18 months. It also required that the paving and upkeep of the street allowance between the tracks would remain the responsibility of the company.

The firm of Von Echo Construction was given the contract to build the railway and the first track was laid July 3, 1900. An order was placed with the Censlager Bros. of Harrisburg, Pa., for a vehicle to furnish travelling accommodation for the street railway. The head office of the company was opened in Woodstock on July 1, 1900, with J. G. Wallace president. The office was located in the McLeod Building opposite the North American Hotel. It was anticipated that eventually this section of the electric street railway would become part of a giant network, linking Niagara Falls and Windsor and provide better service and accommodation than the steam railways which at that time skirted most communities.

The long awaited street car arrived in Woodstock on a flat car. People made all sorts of excuses to go down to the G. W. R. Station just to view the new car. The majority of the viewers felt a little disappointed in what they saw. Instead of the large elaborate parlor type car which they expected, they saw a small, but ornate car (Toonerville Trolley Type). The main body of the car was decorated with a rustic design and the name "Estelle" in bold letters immediately caught the eye of the viewers. A vestibule at either end served as a loading or unloading platform, along with accommodation for the conductor and any surplus baggage that could not be accommodated on the inside. The controls could be operated from either end depending on the direction of travel. Above the main body of the Estelle there was a transom which was gaily decorated with small windows of coloured glass, above which was the trolley rod which supplied the path for the electricity to travel from the overhead line to the motor of the street car.

Inside, in place of the plush seats that were expected, there appeared two benches along either side capable of accommodating 24 passengers. During the peak periods extra passengers were allowed to stand.

For the comfort of the travelling public during adverse weather a small pot-bellied stove occupied a corner inside the coach. As with all stoves of this vintage it could not be relied upon to furnish an even degree of heat throughout the car. Instead it would often baulk and instead of heat would belch out smoke and almost asphyxiate the passengers. Other days it would refuse to burn and the passengers would nearly freeze, while on milder days it would be necessary to leave the doors open to allow the heat to escape and make breathing possible.

Many of the curious wondered why this street car should be named "Estelle". No answer was forthcoming but eventually it was learned that Dr. Ickes' daughter had the same name.

The original line started at Wellington St. and proceeded down Dundas St. to Mill. Later the line was extended east to Huron St. At Mill St. the line proceeded south to Park Row and out to the Ingersoll Road and Fairmont Park, Beachville and Ingersoll.

The youth of the day considered the trip down Dundas St. hill a source of entertainment as it was always a question, "Would Estelle make the curve?" Just in case she would make the curve at Mill and Dundas some brave young buck would run up behind the car and pull the trolley off the overhead line and leave Estelle at the mercy of the foot brakes, which required sand to help stop her progress. As a result she quite frequently left the rail.

There was always the problem of climbing this hill on the return trip. On different occasions passengers had been asked to disembark and walk up the hill in order for Estelle to make the grade. During the winter of 1901 when Estelle had considerable trouble on the hill and other grades, the company decided to purchase a snow plow. For the benefit of those not being able to enjoy the antics of Estelle, the local press daily reported any unusual happenings aboard her.

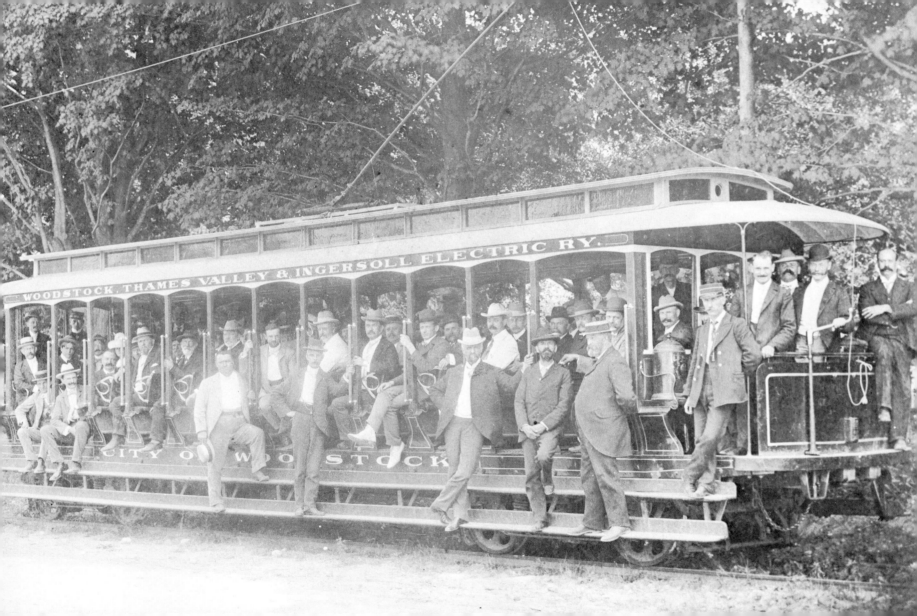

On preceding page — "The City of Woodstock" shortly after her inaugural run. Above — A scene on the Thames at Fairmont Park in 1902. On facing page — What appears to be a tug-of-war is really what was a common sight on Dundas Street. In the spring or after a heavy rainstorm, mud got so deep that it affected the operation of "The City of Woodstock". Assistance was provided by the steam roller. The setting is looking east from Griffin's Opera House.

The last car out on Saturday night was a ride to remember, as all the revellers made for home after a night on the town, and each added his share of entertainment to what would have otherwise been a monotonous journey with passengers falling asleep and missing their stop. Of course Estelle would stop for anybody at any time, once it left the city limits.

The original run stopped at Beachville. This was caused by a delay in obtaining the franchise held by the Ingersoll Radio Electric Company. The railway committee of the Ontario Legislature ordered the Ingersoll Company to surrender its franchise to the Woodstock, Thames Valley and Ingersoll Street Railway and work progressed to Ingersoll. The first trip to Ingersoll was in June, 1901. It had been the intention of the company to extend its lines to Embro and West Zorra but when the citizens voted on the question it was turned down. Embro voted in favour of the line. It was also requested that the company extend their lines in Woodstock to include both railway stations. The company declined, claiming that the expense of $5,000 a mile was far greater than the runs would return in revenue.

The line was progressive and as a promotional scheme, land along the Thames River was obtained and a recreation area was prepared. This became known as "Fairmont Park", this name being taken from Fairmont Park, Penn., the home state of the original promoters.

In order to accommodate more passengers to and from the park, a second car was added. This was known as the "City of Woodstock". It was an open type car with seating room for considerably more passengers. The car was used during the summer and remained in the shed when not in use.

Fairmont Park became the haven for all lovers of the great out-of-doors. The Bohemian Club established a camp at the park. Stuart Dawes, Jack Flyn, Bill Phillips, George Price, Bob Coles, J. Sutherland, Bert Potts and Chas. Smith were among its members.

A pavilion was erected amid a grove of trees and a small summer stock company came to town each summer and entertained with three performances a week. The local orchestra conducted by Frank Windsor held weekly dances.

On the banks of the Thames, a boathouse was erected and canoes were rented. Many of those who did their courting at the turn of the century recall pleasant memories of paddling down the river with a young lady in the front seat. Parties were often arranged and would meet in some secluded cove. Of course, a banjo player was always present and all the latest songs of the day such as Moonlight Bay, In the Good Old Summer Time and others would be sung as the moonlight filtered through the willows on the young at heart.

Today this is all just a memory and the polluted Thames no longer lures the young lovers. The old "Estelle" and the "City of Woodstock" have gone and the tracks have been removed. After a quarter of a century of service the line ceased to operate and in 1925 was replaced by buses. Today the Blue Bird buses are also a memory.

The final chapter of the Woodstock, Thames Valley and Ingersoll Street Railway was written in January 1939, when the office of the company was officially closed. This last link with Estelle, while containing the office of the president of the firm, also served as the waiting room and the conductors' quarters. It was also the gathering place for families when a trip to town was made by a family from out along the rails.

In 1937, long after she was retired from service, "The City of Woodstock" provided these girls with a place to play "Toonerville Trolley".

Upper left is a view of the Thames Valley just south of Woodstock as it appeared in 1903. The road running through the picture is what is now Hwy. #2 and between the road and the near fence can be seen the tracks used by the "Estelle" and "The City of Woodstock". Towards the upper left of the photo one can see the three rail lines running through this portion of the valley. Upper right — Fairmont Park, looking west across the Thames.

The following is an advertisement which appeared in the Sentinel-Review on April 1st, 1881. It was placed in the paper by Nicholson, the Photographer.

Should auld acquaintance be forgot
    An' never brought to mind?
Should folk no gie their Photographs
    To friens o' auld lang syne?

Then come awa', friens, one an' all,
    An' dinna lose no time
In getting pictures for your friens —
    For Nicholson takes them fine.

An' if ye dinna ken the place,
    Try Parker's an' Hood's to fin',
Ye'll see him up twa flights o' stairs —
    As in days o' auld lang syne.

An' when ye get a score or twa,
    Let ane o' them be mine,
To mind me o' the cantie days
    We had ib auld lang syne.

For we're growin' auld an' nearin 'fast
    The hame that's yours an' mine,
Then let our friens see how we lookit
    In the days o' auld lang syne.

For surely you'll be your phisog,
    An' surely I'll be mine,
An' we'll let our friens see how we lookit
    In days o' auld lang syne.

WOODSTONIANS AND THEIR CARS

On facing page — In 1917, the big event of the week was the "Sunday Afternoon Drive". This page — These photos of bicycles (standard, deluxe and super-deluxe models) depict owners as proud of their vehicles as those who owned cars a few years later. Upper left — Shy but proud, these ladies show off a 1900 super-deluxe cruiser. Lower left — Dad and Mom can clown, but the bicycle is all-important to daughter. Upper right — The A. S. Ball family (and bicycle) posed for this photo in 1899. Lower right — A messenger boy pedals past Sid Coppins' plumbing shop in 1894.

This page — On the left is A. W. Shaver's motor delivery truck, the first of its kind in Woodstock. It was built in this city at Oxford Motors by Frank Craig and Gordon Marr. Below is the 1902 Oldsmobile owned by Sid Coppins. This was the second automobile to appear in Woodstock. On facing page — At the top are three views of Craig McKay's 1906 Oldsmobile. The lower left photo shows Sid Coppins (right) who owned automobiles for almost sixty consecutive years, proudly posing with a new acquisition early in the century. Lower right — Many people would pay five times the original price of about $1,000 for this 1915 beauty.

1902

On facing page — Upper left: "Home, James, and don't spare the horses." Upper right: "All packed and and ready for the road." Lower left and right — A picnic at Southside Park just wasn't a picnic without the family car in attendance. Above left — In 1927, as now, cars, crowds and a parade made for noisy, happy times. This photo, taken during the Old Boys' Reunion of that year, shows a boisterous reception on Finkle St. at Dundas. Above right — As automobiles increased in number, so did the quality of existing roads. Thus ended the true pioneer era of motoring.

ONTARIO HOSPITAL, WOODSTOCK

This hospital has been one of the steadily expanding facilities in this area. Since its official opening in 1906, the land area has increased from 100 to 617 acres; the buildings from an Administration Building and two Cottages, providing accommodation for 80 patients, to twenty-six Wards and Cottages, with accommodation for 1500 patients; and from a mere handful of staff to a complement of 765 employees, with an annual payroll of over three and a half million dollars. This hospital was originally designated for the care and treatment of persons suffering from epilepsy, but as of 1939 it became a hospital of two Divisions, the Epilepsy Division on the west side of Highway 59 with accommodation for 603 patients, and the Chest Diseases Division on the east side of the Highway for the treatment of tuberculous mentally ill and mentally retarded, with accommodation for 895 patients.

In 1903, one hundred acres of land was purchased by the Ontario Government from Charles S. Hatch, and this became the core of the present hospital. The Administration Building is located almost on the site of the Hatch Homestead, on the crest of a hill overlooking the Thames River Valley. The Chest Diseases Division is located on a hill which now overlooks the lake created by the Gordon Pittock Dam.

Construction of the buildings started in 1904, and the first patient was admitted on April 22, 1906, with Dr. J. J. Williams as the first Superintendent. By 1907 the hospital consisted of the Administration Building and four self-contained Cottages, each with its own heating system, kitchen and dining room, and provided accommodation for 200 patients. In that same year, an earth-filled dam was constructed across the creek in the valley west of the hospital buildings, backing up the water to cover about an acre of land, and being nine to eleven feet deep. This was used for boating in the summer, for skating in the winter, and also provided the supply of block ice for the hospital prior to the advent of refrigeration. The dam was washed away in a Spring flood about ten years later and was never replaced.

On Page 156 — The original Administration Building opened in 1906 and is still in contant use. Above, left — The Recreation Hall, opened in 1916, is part of the Epilepsy Division. Above, right — This is Cottage "A", Epilepsy Division. On Page 159 — Functional and modern, this is the New Building, Chest Diseases Division.

Construction over the next few years consisted of residences for the Farm Manager, the Gardener, the Superintendent, a greenhouse, coach house, barns, and finally a recreation hall in 1916. There was no further structural change until 1931, when two ward buildings for patients of two stories each, a central kitchen and dining hall, power house, and laundry and central stores building were opened. Patient accommodation increased from 200 to 600.

In 1939 a new unit for the treatment of children suffering from epilepsy was opened on the east side of Highway 59, with accommodation for 325 children. Some one hundred children were admitted, but with the advent of World War II and the taking over of the Ontario Hospital, St. Thomas, by the Royal Canadian Air Force, it was closed as a Children's Unit and became the nucleus of the present Chest Diseases Division, with accommodation for 600 patients, it being necessary to turn classrooms and playrooms into dormitories. This increased the bed capacity from 600 to 1200.

In 1958 a new four-storey building was added to the Chest Diseases Division which had a bed capacity of 566, and contained many new facilities which now serve both Divisions of the hospital. This was the first opportunity available to remove the extra beds which caused considerable overcrowding, leaving a total bed capacity for 1500 patients. A new Mechanical Trades Building was completed and opened for operation the same year. Since then there have been no major changes to the hospital, other than in-hospital structural alterations and the addition of new services.

The hospital today provides many services which are of great benefit to the surrounding area, and the province as a whole. The Mental Health Clinic and Day-Care Centre, opened in 1950, serve the County of Oxford in providing treatment, guidance and rehabilitation for out-patients. The Neurophysiology Department does diagnostic electroencephalograms on patients in this hospital, as well as patients from nearby Ontario Hospitals, and out-patients on referral by private practitioners. The Chest Clinic, located in the Chest Diseases Division, operates the anti-tuberculosis control program for all hospitals in Ontario under the Mental Health Branch, including Ontario Hospitals, Ontario Hospital Schools, and Mental Retardation Assessment Centres. A total of approximately 50,000 chest X-ray films on some 46,000 individuals are interpreted in the Chest Clinic each year. X-ray technicians from the Clinic travel to the various hospitals to assist in the annual chest X-ray survey, and, in addition, specially qualified physicians from the Clinic visit the hospitals twice yearly to do necessary physical examinations and tuberculin testing, where indicated, following their interpretation of the X-rays. The hospital also provides clinical experience and academic training in Psychiatry for the student nurses of the Woodstock General Hospital.

A small laboratory, occupying one room and with one technician, was started in 1939 when the Chest Diseases Division opened. This became an Associate Laboratory in 1946, a Regional Laboratory in 1956, and the Public Health Laboratory in 1966, and now occupies thirteen rooms with a personnel of twenty-one, and serves the Counties of Oxford, Brant, Norfolk and Haldimand.

Of the present hospital property, there are now 400 acres under cultivation for fruit, vegetables and grain. This provides sufficient fresh produce for hospital use. During 1965, the dairy herd of pure-bred Holstein-Friesian cattle was discontinued, the old dairy barns demolished, a new pole barn erected, and beef cattle replaced the dairy herd. Milk is now purchased from area farmers and processed in the hospital pasteurization plant.

The hospital has an additional impressive list of medical services available, including diagnostic X-ray, Occupational Therapy Departments, Industrial Therapy Departments, Physiotherapy Departments, a Rehabilitation Department, a Social Service Department, electrocardiography, full-time dental services, full-time chaplaincy service, a furnished apartment for the educational program in domestic science, libraries for patients, and a well-equipped medical library.

For physical therapy and recreational purposes, there are four softball diamonds, a tennis court, a bowling green, a golf course, and miniature golf courses on the hospital grounds, and four large indoor recreational areas.

In 1959 a Women's Auxiliary to the Ontario Hospital, with Mrs. Spencer Hunter as the first President, was organized. This Auxiliary has been of great benefit to the patients by interesting local organizations and citizens in drawing the patients into the life of the community.

PRESERVING OUR CANADIAN HERITAGE

During the crucial years prior to Confederation, many meetings were held to discuss the possibilities of Canada and the British colonies of New Brunswick, Nova Scotia and Prince Edward Island and Newfoundland joining together as one country. In 1854 a meeting, now known as "The Charlottetown Conference", was held in Charlottetown, P.E.I. This meeting and one held in Quebec are considered the two most important meetings held prior to Confederation in 1867.

Since that time, Sir John A. Macdonald and his colleagues have gone to their reward and are remembered as "The Fathers of Confederation". Now all that remains is the building and the chamber they met in. Most important of all are the chairs and tables they occupied during their discussions. The building has become a memorial to Confederation and the chamber, while neglected for many years, has been restored to its original dignity. But in 1952 the furniture had been left to slowly fade away.

It appeared that the furniture would soon have to be removed and an important link with our Canadian Heritage would be lost, less than 100 years following this momentous meeting.

A family from Woodstock visited Charlottetown during the summer of 1952 and called at Confederation Chamber. Being interested in Canada's heritage, the sight they saw depressed them. The guide, while apologizing for the condition of the furniture, claimed that little could be done to preserve it as funds were not available.

"Do you think it would be possible for an interested individual to start a fund for their preservation?" asked the visitor.

The guide excused himself and returned shortly with an invitation to accompany him to the office of Premier Jones.

The visitor introduced himself as Mr. V. B. King of Woodstock, Ontario. The two gentlemen discussed at great length the procedure to be followed so the work of restoring the furniture could be accomplished and that any interested party could contribute to a fund to pay for restoring the furniture to its original beauty.

Premier Jones and Mr. King went to the office of Charlottetown's leading newspaper, "The Guardian" and explained their intentions to Mr. Frank Walker, the associate editor. He agreed with them, and offered to give all the publicity possible to create an interest and to receive contributions for the fund. The date was July 2, 1952, with Canada's Centennial Year still fifteen years away.

It was left in the hands of Premier Jones and Mr. Walker with the understanding that any expense over the amount raised would be borne by Mr. King. Work was to begin immediately.

The correspondence which followed indicated that it might be necessary for the furniture to be sent to the United States for the restoration work. Mr. King strongly disagreed with this and stated that if the work could not be done in the Maritimes he would arrange to have it done in Ontario. Following up his request, Preston Fraser, a native of P.E.I., now living in New Glasgow, N.S., was located and agreed to do the job.

The chairs were to be sent in small lots to his shop as a precaution against loss or serious damage. The three tables were to be completed in Charlottetown.

Work progressed and by January 16, 1953, twenty-four chairs had been completely restored and returned. One table had been restored and an extra leg applied to relieve some of the sagging.

The speech from the throne opening the Third Session of the Forty-Eighth General Assembly of the Province of Prince Edward Island on March 3, 1953, made mention of the work done on the Confederation furniture, mentioning Mr. V. B. King of Woodstock, as the inspiration behind the project.

The work was completed in time to be included in the fiscal year ending in March, 1953. During this period, July 2, 1952, to March 1, 1953, the public had shown little interest in the project. The result was that Mr. King contributed the entire amount needed to preserve an important link in our Canadian heritage, and to show that we in Woodstock are proud of our Canadian heritage, no matter where it is located in Canada.

WOODSTOCK IN THE 1920'S

During the 1920's Woodstock's population was in the 10,000 bracket and in 1927, at the time of the Old Boys' Reunion, it had reached 10,200 and its assessment that year was $8,000,000 for all purposes. It was classed as being in the heart of Industrial Western Ontario. An overnight trip on the train would place you in Ottawa, Montreal, New York or Boston. Cleveland, Detroit and Chicago were practically next door neighbours.

For local connections it was possible to travel on branch lines to St. Thomas, St. Marys, Port Dover or Stratford in a matter of hours. The province's leading highway, King's Highway #2, passed through the heart of the city and supplied ideal conditions for those who preferred to travel or ship via highway transport service.

Along this highway came a new phase in the life of Woodstock's residents — tourists. The country was alive with people who were anxious to travel now that Henry Ford had made the Model T available to the working man. People were turning their spare rooms into dollars by renting these rooms, advertising their homes as "Tourist Homes". The cities were also anxious to have these tourists stop over so tourist camps came into being. Woodstock had one of the first of these tourist camps, at Southside Park. A completely electric kitchen was furnished free of charge for all who used the park.

On Pages 161 through 165 — If you turn these pages slowly you will realize that you are looking at not three, but one, unique photograph. It was taken in 1927 with a panoramic camera which was placed directly in front of the City Hall. The camera was aimed north and the mechanism started. As it slowly rotated to the east, south, west and back to north, it passed through 365 degrees, the result of which you see on these pages. Right — Store window displays were gaudy in the 20's as were the ties. This is Grafton's Father's Day window in 1929. Far Right — Shows the interior of the B. J. Rae & Son printing office (now the Commercial Print-Craft) in 1927. Among the employees shown are the present owners of Commercial Print-Craft, T. M. Young and G. L. Tait.

Swimming and playground facilities were available, and dances and band concerts were held in the pavilion. This, along with the ample amount of shade trees in the area, made Woodstock a mecca for tourists.

Industry has always played an important part in the life of the city. In the 1920's, Woodstock was producing automobile parts, agriculture implements, batteries, boxes, braid, boilers, biscuits, casters,

concrete pipe, car liners, churns, cider, dairy machinery, draperies, electric generators and appliances, hosiery, woollen goods, fire engines, furnaces, furniture, flour, garden implements, curtain rods, pipe and reed organs, road machinery, stoves, sewing machines, shoes, rubber footwear and wagons, to name but a few.

The names and buildings used by many of these firms have passed out of the picture. Today they are only a memory of the era when

$3.20 was a good day's pay. The site of Woodstock's greatest industry, "Canada Furniture Manufacturers Ltd.", now houses an apple storage plant, a warehouse for Harvey Woods Ltd., and a bowling alley. Murray & Maclean still use the office building and deal in lumber, the remnants of the successor of the furniture company, Wood Mosaic. All that remains of the Woodstock Wagon Works is an old building with a faded out sign "Home of Buster Brown Wagons" on Ingersoll Rd. Eureka is still a name but no longer are they turning out planters and lawnmowers; they have been absorbed by Kelsey Hayes. Their neighbours, James Stewart and Crown Lumber have gone, but still mail is received for Stewart which has to be forwarded to Penetanguishene. The Thomas Organ Co. is just a name and large portions of the buildings have been removed.

The Bain Wagon Works, later Massey Ferguson, is among the last of the oldtimers to leave town. A shopping centre is rising on this site on Dundas St. Before they left for Brantford, Massey Ferguson presented the city fathers with a substantial cheque to be used in preserving the City Hall.

Bickle Fire Engines has been replaced by King Seagrave Ltd. who revived the fire engine trade. The site of the Concrete Pipe Co. is now a large groceteria.

Industry has changed, and so have businesses on Dundas St. Among leading merchants that are no longer to be found here are names like John White, which is now Walkers Dept. Store, and the Princess and Griffin theatres which have been replaced by the Capitol Theatre. The E. J. Coles store, later Canadian Department Stores and then Eaton's, is now Beamish Dept. Store. The site of the old Y.M.C.A. is now the new home of Canada Permanent, and Berlette's Car Sales is the site of the new Bank of Montreal. The Sentinel-Review, now a Thomson newspaper, and no longer the publisher of "Rod and Gun", has moved from Dundas St. to Brock St.

The passing of time creates many changes in a community, often for the better. While many old names have been removed, others remain but under new names, while still others have come to replace the departed. This is known as Progress.

In the spring of 1881, "General" Butler, a negro handyman, placed the following advertisement in the Sentinel-Review:

De ole hen am chirpin',
De robin am singin',
De voice of de rooster
Am heard in de land.

De mud's growin' deeper,
De sewer's a'diggin',
De rats am a'comin' out
Ob de cellar to see.

De pigeons am flyin',
De ganders am sighin',
An' de big Town Constable
Am showin' his hand.

De lambs am a'callin',
De spring calf am bawlin',
An' de white wash season
Has opened for me.

Wheneber you're feelin'
It's time for house cleanin',
Jest send round your boy
For the General, that's me.

My office's down below,
De Port Dover Rail Row,
On de fust street, turn norf,
Come an' see.

Above — "General" Grant and his two helpers stand in front of his workshop on June 15th, 1898. The "General" (not to be confused with "General" Butler in the poem above) may also be seen on Page 45. Right — Everybody loves a parade and the year 1900 was no exception. These scenes are on Dundas at Graham St. looking east. The Caister House was located at that time on the site of the present Bank of Commerce. On facing page — Right Side — This is the Bain Wagon Works Fire Department in 1908 (bottom) and in 1915 (top). Lower left — Woodstock's first motor taxi was made at the Woodstock Auto Manufacturing Co. plant on Mill St. in 1912. Upper left — Bert Hick's taxi in 1915.

168

WILLIAM GREY, WOODSTOCK'S THIRD MAYOR

William Grey came to Woodstock when the community was still referred to as "The Town Plot". He saw the village grow, expand into a town and become a city in 1901. He was the third mayor of the Town and held this position several times later. Two Woodstock subdivisions and Grey Memorial Hall at New St. Paul's Church perpetuate his name.

Mr. Grey was born on October 18, 1812, at West Pennard, Somersetshire, England. His father migrated to Canada in 1818, followed the following year by his wife and family. They first settled at Nicolet in Lower Canada and came to Oxford in 1825. They made their home a few miles east of Woodstock. When Wm. Grey erected his own residence, it was located at the corner of Buller and Graham Sts., on the site of the present armoury. In 1840 he built the first three-storey brick building in the village ,the Royal Pavilion Hotel, which for many years was considered to be the finest in the area within fifty miles of Woodstock. A public spirited citizen, he advanced the interests of Woodstock in many ways and his financial acumen was recognized by the directors of the Oxford Permanent, of which he served as president from 1865 until February 25, 1897.

He was an active member of New St. Paul's Church and a very close friend of Rev. J. C. Farthing, who later became Bishop of Montreal. Wm. Grey left the church a considerable part of his estate at his death. This was to be used first for the purchase of a set of chimes and secondly to make necessary repairs to the schoolroom. The latter bequest was used to build Grey Memorial Hall.

A city subdivision west of Mill St. and south of Joint is called the Wm. Grey subdivision as is another, located west of Givins St. He was an active worker in getting the hospital started here and endowed a ward which bears his name.

Mr. Wm. Grey, a leading figure in the early life of Woodstock, died March 23, 1904.

THE OXFORD BUILDING AND SAVINGS SOCIETY

This Society was formed in 1865 primarily for the purpose of encouraging the accumulation of capital, provide a safe and permanent investment for the same and to raise a fund from which the owners of real estate might obtain a loan on the security of their property.

Originally known as the "Royal Farmers Savings Society" until October 27, 1865, when Wm. Grey was elected president and the name changed to Oxford Permanent Building and Savings Society. Wm. Grey remained as president until 1897, a period of more than 31 years, and was an influential party in the achievements of the Society.

The secretary was instructed in 1878 to place notices in the local papers "That the Society was prepared to receive money for deposit. On demand deposits up to $200, it would pay 5% and on deposits up to $2,000, withdrawals on 90 days notice, the rate was 6%." The president and secretary-treasurer were instructed in 1877 to take the necessary steps to bring the business of the Society more prominently before the public.

During these early years the directors set a pattern of austere frugality. The salary of the secretary-treasurer, C. L. Beard, was originally set at $400, but in 1868 it was cut to $200. The following year it was decided to give him a yearly raise of $50. In 1877 he was barred from taking a commission on stock. In 1877 the shareholders voted $300 to the president as a slight acknowledgment of his services. Annual reports made their appearance in 1875. In 1872 they voted $16.50 to the president and secretary for a business trip to Windsor; the following year they voted $2.00 a day for attendance at board meetings. The solicitor of the Society was instructed in 1879 "that in future all mortgages payable to this Society be made in gold or its equivalent".

The first loan entered on the books was on March 6, 1866, to Jas. N. Nasmyth, for $350 on security of Lot 6 on the east side of Vansittart

Ave. On the same date, Mrs. Ellen Smith Kay obtained $200 on a house and lot on Brock St. Thereafter, the board met and approved loans for residents in all parts of the county and in December, 1869, a loan was made to Michael Hogan of Wyoming in Lambton County to be the first made outside the county.

Many loans were made on farm property which frequently included log cabins. A loan was approved to Charles Cassidy of Dereham for $200 for two years on the security of a log house, frame barn, 60 acres of cleared land and 57 acres of bush. Alex McDonald of Lot 13, Concession 9, East Zorra, obtained $1,500 on his property containing a house, barn, stable and 70 acres of cleared land.

It was building time in town and many investors in Woodstock augmented their capital with the co-operation of the Society. The building on the northwest corner of Graham and Dundas is probably the one planned by Robert Woodroofe, "132 by 22, three storeys in front 30 feet, and remainder two storeys, to cost not less than $6,000", and on which he applied for a loan of $8,000 for five years at $6\frac{1}{2}\%$.

George Harwood got a loan to help build a new store in the church block. This evidently meant the Dundas - Light - Hunter - Graham block which had been originally set apart for the Anglican Church in Woodstock. When Old St. Paul's was built, this church land was gradually sold in lots. Wm. Bishop got a loan of $600 on the security of a hotel and stables on the west side of Graham St., described as being on the "church survey".

The Society was also willing to loan money to churches. In 1878 the rector and wardens of St. Paul's Church obtained a loan of $20,000 for 20 years at 8%. Several years later the rector, Rev. James J. Hill and Warden W. A. VanIngen got a reduction in the interest rate to 7% on the then unpaid balance of $15,000.

New St. Paul's was not the only church assisted. In Woodstock the Baptist Institute (Woodstock College) received aid, Willis Church in Clinton got a loan for $5,000 for five years, and the congregation of Innerkip Methodist Church obtained $800 toward construction of a new church 32 by 50 feet to cost $1,000.

The first meeting of the directors was held at the office of Wm. Grey. This could have been at his home on Graham St., the present site of the armoury, or it could have been in one of the many buildings that he owned at that time. It was not until 1874 that the Society acquired a site for a building which it erected the following year at a total cost of $7,641.28 which included the price of the land. Rental of part of the building not occupied by the Society was set at $580 a year. Mr. McQueen obtained two rooms for the Division Court at a rental of $120 a year with the tenant paying the taxes. Later, the Oddfellows had lodge rooms here.

Colleagues of Mr. Grey in the first Oxford Permanent Board included Jas. Scarff, vice-president, Sanford Yale, John Douglas, Thomas Oliver and H. P. Brown with Charles L. Beard as secretary-treasurer. Hugh Richardson was solicitor. Adam Gordon and John White joined later. Strange as it may seem, important members of the elite British Society who settled in Woodstock are not to be found on the Society's records. Some of Admiral Vansittart's children are listed as shareholders in 1890 but their residence was given as England.

The first agent of the Society was Claudius Tidy of Norwich and as a result of this appointment there was an increase in loan applications in that area. Shortly afterwards, agents were appointed in the leading communities of the county.

From little acorns mighty oaks appear. Today, after a very humble, homespun beginning, the Society is continuing to thrive and join forces with other leaders in the field. It is now part of the Canada Permanent Toronto General Trust Corporation and still the leading trust and mortgage firm in Woodstock.

On Page 172 — Woodstock Collegiate Institute in 1914. On Page 173 — Our Public Schools in 1914 were strong, stout functional buildings. Top row, left to right, are Princess, Broadway and Chapel Schools, while below we see Central (with its tower) and Victoria Schools.

172

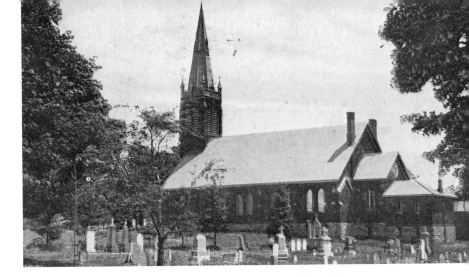

Woodstock is fortunate to be blessed with many fine churches of all denominations. Here are five. On the facing page is Knox Presbyterian Church in 1914. This photo was taken from the lawn of the Collegiate and gives a view of the church we will probably never see again. Above is the interior of Old St. Paul's Anglican Church as it appeared about 1907. Below is Chalmers United Church, a beautiful building on spacious grounds. Upper right — St. Mary's Roman Catholic Church and its cemetery (later removed to Highway 2) in 1912. Lower right — New St. Paul's Anglican Church before Grey Memorial Hall was built.

RESIDENTIAL WOODSTOCK

Woodstock's location and topography lend themselves to making an attractive city. Though the situation is high, Woodstock is really situated in a valley or basin with the Thames River entering at the north and Cedar Creek at the south, the two uniting and flowing through the valley to the west. On the southeasterly rim of this basin the first house was erected. Daniel Burtch, in choosing this site for his home, displayed the vision of a seer as all the surrounding countryside could be viewed from there.

Along the same ridge and sloping grade to the northwest, were erected many of the first homes by country gentlemen, who became prominently identified with life and interests of Woodstock and Oxford County. Among the builders of homes on this site we find the names of Dr. Blaquiers, Capt. Drew, Old St. Paul's rectory of Canon Bettridge, the Mills, Cottles, Fauquiers and Alexanders.

At that time the main part of Woodstock was located in the east end. The first brick house was built in 1836 and was located to the west of the old rectory. It was followed by a second in 1837 which was built by George Elliott. George Gray built the first three-storey building which was a hotel known as the Royal Pavilion. It was built in front of the courthouse in West Woodstock in 1844 at a cost of 500 pounds ($1,500 today). An ever increasing number of homes were built, many of which were architectural masterpieces. Many can still be seen on Vansittart Avenue, in the area between Graham and Oxford Streets and Dundas and Ingersoll Avenue, in the east end on Wilson St. or in its immediate vicinity, and in the area around Old St. Paul's Church.

Some of these stand out, such as the old T. L. Wilson home on Vansittart Avenue and Alex Watson's home. An example of the excellent workmanship is displayed on Wilson Street at the old D. W. Karn home. A wing on the north side of this house was removed in one piece and placed on a foundation on the south side to form a separate house, with no ill effects. Considering the size of this wing, very few would attempt the task today, especially if it was going to involve a 20th century home.

It was not unusual in those days to have walls three bricks thick and the foundation floor to rest on 2" x 12" timbers running the full length of the structure, in one piece. Today it would be considered a waste of time, money and material to build in this manner. In days gone by, these homes were a mark of social prominence and class distinction which the passing years have erased. These homes were surrounded by a fair acreage which necessitated the use of a gardener and handyman to keep the property up to the Joneses.

Since then, great strides have been made in the number and character of Woodstock's homes. In the early days the style wasn't always modern or attractive but, in recent years, the trend has been to smaller and more modern dwellings and the location has been more tasteful with parts of the town being made residential and other parts set aside for industry.

One of the first sections set aside for a residential area was in the northeast section, which became known as the Huron Park Development project. The property known as the Tobin farm was purchased in 1947 during the term of Mayor Charles Burston and the first sod turned. This area was laid out to have the homes built in such a way as to not obstruct the view of its neighbour.

When it came to naming the streets in new areas it was realized that Old London had a soft spot in the hearts of many just returning from the war, and it was decided to rename Knights Road, Knightsbridge Road after a familiar name in South Kensington. Off this street one can find other streets such as Grosvenor, Earlscourt, Brompton, Sloane, Cromwell, Berwick, Belgrave, Warwick, Wilton, Kensington.

All streets were not so named, as Mayor Bernadette Smith named Jubilee and Vimy Place. Other streets were named by developers after members of their families. Brenda Crescent is named after the daughter of R. G. Thompson.

As new sections of this residential area were opened, many more streets had to be named. Many of the contractors followed the old pattern and named them in honour of outstanding citizens such as Dent Street after Thomas Dent, M.L.A.; McKenzie after Mayor Edward McKenzie; Hayball after Mayor Charles Hayball; Lee to honour Arthur Lee, the former town clerk; and George Miller is remembered by

Miller Street. West Street is named after a former Mayor. Parkinson recalls a noted family. We also find names of world figures such as Field Marshal Alexander with Alexander St., and Winston Churchill with Churchill Place. Other streets have taken on colourful names such as Orchard, Briarhill, Heather, Edgewood which all go to make a new area more appealing, but the trend remains to honour the outstanding citizens.

Looking over the present trend, we find that Woodstock appears to be in its second cycle of progressive expansion. The original town was in the east end and the first cycle of expansion carried it to the west and now we find it returning to the east. This time the city is expanding in an orderly fashion and the old idea of class distinction has completely disappeared.

CHECKERBOARD SQUARE IS WOODSTOCK

Ralston Purina of Canada Ltd. represents forty years of progress to Woodstock, forty years contributed to Canada's spectacular growth in agriculture and food production. Woodstock is Checkerboard Square, the head offices for this world famous trademark of quality— The Checkerboard. George E. Pierce, president, in remarking on the history of the company, states, "It is a business success story of growing big by remaining small, of producing for basic wants, for a better human livelihood, by revolutionizing the production of meat, milk and eggs. Purina is the recognized leader in getting 'more from what we have' in Canadian agriculture — a slogan in the past which has become a necessity of the future. Food is our business!"

When the company first opened its doors for business January 2, 1928, it employed three office and eighteen mill employees. One, J. W. "Bill" Harris, continues today as a loyal employee. It is interesting to note that five present employees have over thirty-five years service, seven have over thirty years, three are in the twenty-five year group, sixteen with twenty years. Added together, today's Woodstock organization of 103 represents over one thousand years of feed manufacturing service. Personal growth, development and welfare of employees has been and continues to be one of the strongest incentives in the company's success and a smallness never to be lost.

Growth in the early years was slow but steady until today the company represents a multi-million dollar business employing 626 Canadians. The chow division has feed manufacturing facilities not only in Woodstock, but also Whitby, Montreal and St. Romuald, Quebec, distributing and serving all Eastern Canada through 454 independently owned Purina franchise dealers, plus three company owned Maritime installations supported by a Purina sales force of fifty-one trained agri-business managers.

Diversification of the operations came in 1962 through the acquisition of Choice Cut-Up Chicken Company Ltd., Aurora, Ontario. This placed the company into the production of broiler meat. Doubling in capacity since that date, the Company is co-operating with The Ontario Broiler Market Board to provide the maximum return to the grower and least cost product to the Ontario housewife through increased efficiency in broiler breeding, hatching, grow-out and processing. Today, wages buy 4.6 lbs. of broiler meat, compared with 3.3 lbs. in 1960.

As recent as mid-1966, turkey meat production was added through the acquisition of Shantz Processing Ltd. and related companies in Ingersoll. Turkey Breeder Research and production, hatching, grow-out and processing facilities are integrated into a growing service industry dedicated to producers and consumers alike. Approximately one hundred Ingersoll and district people find gainful employment in this new and expanding industry, which in the coming year will contribute in excess of half a million dollars to the local economy through payroll, supplies, taxes and utilities.

Dog chow and cat chow, the leading Canadian dry pet food products, were the reason for the company's 1960 investment in special plant and equipment at Clarkson, Ontario. Operating through chain and grocery stores, kennels and pet stores, the grocery division distributes from coast to coast an ever widening range of pet food products — dog meal, tuna for cats, and dairy dinner. Soon to be packed in Canada will be the many quality "Chicken of the sea" tuna products from Purina's Van Camp Division. This will later include shrimp and king crab.

The Standard Wire Fence Company plant as it appeared in 1905.

In planning for the future, Ralston Purina of Canada Ltd. has set as its attainable five-year goal, to become a $100,000,000 business dedicated to providing the necessary services and products to assure agricultural stability through effectively meeting customer demand for food.

Commenting on the local operations, L. H. Stringham, vice-president of chow production, states, "The Woodstock plant today manufactures and ships more tons of quality Purina Chows in two weeks than it did during its first full year of production forty years ago. As a matter of fact, better than a fifth of the prepared feeds used by Ontario farmers is produced right here at Checkerboard Square."

The Woodstock Mill is one of the largest and busiest feed manufacturers in Canada. Though annual corn receipts from local farmers means over $800,000 to Oxford County cash farm income, its contribution is not limited to agriculture alone. Ralston Purina of Canada Ltd. locally contributes better than $110,000 for utilities; supplies and stationery in excess of $75,000; salaries and wages well over $500,000. A total of more than $750,000 is pumped into the economy of Woodstock alone.

Woodstock and Oxford County have a real partner in progress in Ralston Purina of Canada Ltd. — growing strong together.

STANDARD TUBE AND T.I. LIMITED

The Company began — in Woodstock — as the Standard Wire Fence Company — back in 1905. The plant was the rented corner of a rather rundown building, but the six employees turned out good woven wire fence that found a ready market.

The first building at the present site of the plant was erected in 1906. It was only 50 feet by 100 feet, but it was progress. While woven wire fence was still the main product, Davis Patent posts and Church fence stretchers were added to the line during the next five years in an endeavour to build volume.

It was decided in the year 1912 that tubular fence posts would round out the line. So the Hamilton Tube Company of Welland was acquired and a 100 foot addition put on the plant to accommodate this new part of the business. The name of the company was changed to Standard Tube and Fence Company. Of course, "butted" tubing was the only kind made, but as well as the fence market, it found a steady sale to the bed manufacturers who used the tubing for spindles and cross bars.

This is a photo taken from the top of "York Knit" chimney about 1925. You are looking north east and can see the Court House, Central School, Knox Church and the Collegiate.

In most companies one event stands out as the beginning of real progress. With Standard Tube it was in 1919 when extensive experimentation was carried on with the acetylene welding of tubing. As a result of this research, the fence part of the business was sold in 1921 and the name of the company changed to Standard Tube Company Limited.

Advancement was steady during the nineteen twenties. A growing list of customers included users of tubular parts for automobiles, aeroplanes, agricultural implements, washing machines and vacuum cleaners as well as users of transformer cooling tubes and bicycle and saw frame tubing.

In 1937, Canada's first electric resistance welded tubing was made at Standard Tube.

The Company was purchased in 1943 by the Canadian owned General Products Mfg. Corporatiodn Limited, London, Ontario.

A connection was formed with Tube Investments of Great Britain in 1951 and the company name changed to Standard Tube and T. I. Limited.

A building devoted exclusively to Micro-Rock, the cold reducing of seamless hollows to finished tubes, was erected in 1953.

A new division (now known as the Special Products Division) was set up in 1936 for the manufacture of products made from the Company's steel tubing. Stacking chairs and tables were introduced to

Canada that same year. In 1938 industrial trucks and shop furniture were added. A separate plant was acquired for this division in 1947. The manufacture of Boat Trailers was commenced in 1954. This developed, in 1959, into the now famous line of Canadian Explorer Boat Trailers.

So 1905's few rented feet of space has, today, turned into well over 400,000 square feet of modern manufacturing facilities; the payroll of six has grown to one of close to 700 employees.

"YORK KNIT"

The firm which has the biggest payroll in the City, Harvey Woods Ltd., was originally three independent firms. Puritan Knitting Mills in Toronto was founded in 1904 by Mr. James Woods, later Sir James Woods. It was founded chiefly to supply Gordon Mackay and Co., a leading wholesale house. In 1911 it became York Knitting Mills.

The mill housed wool and cotton yarn spinning, the knitting of fabrics, and the production of a wide range of underwear. In the early 1920's the company introduced a range of high grade underwear to the retail trade through an associated sales company, The Woods Underwear Company.

During the same general period the Zimmerknit Company in Hamilton came to the fore. It made similar products to those made by York Knitting Mills and sold to the wholesale trade. The senior officers of Zimmerknit were killed in a level crossing accident and the company was taken over by Mr. K. W. Harvey of Woodstock, who had established two companies here. These were Hosiers Limited and the Harvey Knitting Company, making an extensive range of hosiery and underwear.

Like many others at the time, this company encountered difficulties during the debacle of 1929 and in 1931 the York Knitting Mills undertook to operate the three mills, two of which had been in competition with York and one of which, the hosiery mill, had been in competition with the Toronto Hosiery Company — another of Sir James Woods' enterprises.

Early in the 1930's the York Knitting Mills' garment production was divided between Hamilton and Woodstock. The Toronto Hosiery Co. operated two factories in Toronto. These were merged and shortly afterwards became part of York Knitting Mills. Their production was moved into the York Knitting Mills plant, filling for a time the space vacated by the underwear manufacturing.

In 1937 the Zimmerknit Company, the Harvey Knitting Company and Hosiers Limited were taken over by York Knitting Mills and a long period of consolidation began. The small York Paper Box Company, part of the York Knitting Mills complex, was closed and moved to Woodstock to merge with the Woodstock Paper Box, to supply boxes to the company's garment factories in Hamilton and Woodstock. The Woods Underwear Company was closed and a larger consolidated selling force handled the products of the several factories.

During the war the company, cramped for space in Woodstock, acquired the plant of the Woodstock Rubber Company and equipped it for hosiery knitting and for the manufacture of Nylon Tricot lingerie.

In 1958 the production of the Zimmerknit factory in Hamilton was moved to the Harvey Underwear Division in Woodstock and the Zimmerknit plant was disposed of. This necessitated the acquiring of warehouse space in Woodstock. This now forms a separate division, leaving the three other Woodstock buildings to office and manufacturing space. The company's head office was moved to Woodstock about ten years ago.

In 1964 York Knitting Mills divested itself of its spinning operations in Toronto and concentrated virtually all of its manufacturing in Woodstock.

It was not until after the war that the Harvey Woods logo emerged as the central brand of the York Knitting Mills. As the company continued to stress high quality products to the consumer, it became more and more apparent that the dissociation of the brand name from the company name was no longer desirable. Thus York Knitting Mills Limited became Harvey Woods Limited in 1966.

The name — especially the name Woods — continues to have great significance in the company. Sir James Woods died in 1941. His son, Mr. J. D. Woods, is chairman of the Board, and his two sons, J. D. Woods Jr., is president and John Woods is vice-president and general manager.

The number of people, mostly women, employed by this firm, totals almost one thousand.

BICKLE SEAGRAVE — KING SEAGRAVE

Some industries passed out of the picture. This one faded away, but faith in his home town inspired Mr. V. B. King to revive this important industry.

In 1906 Mr. R. S. Bickle founded the R. S. Bickle Company to manufacture fire fighting apparatus. Originally located in Winnipeg, the operations of this firm were moved to Woodstock in 1914. The firm operated at that time in the Woodstock Automobile Company plant at the corner of Mill and Main Streets where Beaver Lumber is presently located. Later operations were moved to Graham Street, where the Bell Telephone is now located.

In 1926 a new plant was built on Young Street and the name of the firm changed to Bickle Fire Engines Limited.

The officers of this firm were Mr. R. S. Bickle, President; Mr. W. R. Bickle, secretary-treasurer, and Mr. B. I. Bickle, sales manager. In 1936 the firm obtained the franchise for the manufacture and sales, in Canada, of the Seagrave Line of Custom Fire Apparatus. It was at this time that the firm name Bickle-Seagrave Limited came into being.

In 1947 the Bickle Brothers sold the firm to a Toronto Syndicate.

In 1952 a new plant was built on No. 2 Highway, where Gardner-Denver are now located. Operations continued here until February of 1956 when the firm ceased operations after 50 years of manufacturing.

In May of 1956, Mr. V. B. King, a prominent local industrialist and a nephew of the original founders of the Bickle Fire Engine Com-

Below, and on the following page — The Old and the New — a 420 I.G.P.M. Pumper built in 1938 by Bickle Seagrave Limited and a modern 1050 I.G.P.M. Combination Pumper built by King Seagrave Limited in their recently built plant in the industrial complex at the north end of the City.

pany, formed a new company to manufacture Fire Fighting apparatus in Woodstock.

This new firm, King Seagrave Limited, while having no connection with its predecessor, did employ many of the key personnel formerly engaged in the manufacturing and sales of fire fighting apparatus.

The new firm was successful in securing the franchise for manufacture and sales of Seagrave Custom Fire Apparatus in Canada.

From a modest beginning in 1956 the firm has recorded steady growth. Operating originally in rented quarters, in 1962 the firm built a new plant on Devonshire Avenue from which modern fire fighting equipment is delivered to municipalities from coast to coast.

The firm has now earned the reputation of the quality leader in this field in Canada.

RADIO STATION CKOX

Radio Station CKOX, owned and operated by the Oxford Broadcasting Company, commenced operation on December 7th, 1947, with studios at 380 Hunter Street. The transmitter is located on the Sweaburg Road one mile south of the Woodstock city limits.

Application for the authority to establish the station in Woodstock was made by M. J. Werry in 1946 before the Board of Governors of the Canadian Broadcasting Corporation who at that time held jurisdiction over such matters. Approval of the application was finally granted in June of 1947 and construction started in September of that year.

Managing Director of the company has been M. J. Werry, a native of Woodstock, who received his B.A. S.C. degree in 1933 from the University of Toronto. He was Chief Engineer, Toronto Studios of the CBC until 1939, was transferred to the CBC head office which he engineered until 1947, when he then resigned to establish the new station in Woodstock.

Studios were maintained at 380 Hunter Street until 1953 when the building at 290 Dundas Street was purchased and modern new studios erected. In 1964 CKOX applied for and received approval for an increase in daytime power from 250 watts to 1000 watts. In May, 1965, the station went on the air with a new antenna system and transmitter. CKOX now provides a good signal during the day from Lake Erie in the south to north of Kitchener, and from London in the west to Brantford in the east.

During the 20 years of its operation, CKOX has carried a number of notable broadcasts. Among these have been speeches and interviews with such personages as Prime Minister Louis St. Laurent, Eleanor Roosevelt, Lester B. Pearson, the visit of Princess Elizabeth and Prince Philip and others.

In addition, they have presented on-the-spot broadcasts of the damage created by the tornado which devastated Sarnia and Lambton County in 1952, Hurricane Hazel and the more than 600 hockey broadcasts which the station has carried since inception. In the same period, CKOX has pioneered in new program formats through the inauguration of programs such as "Party Line", "Trading Post" and the Oxford County Ranch House which have retained a loyal and increasing audience through the years.

GARDNER-DENVER COMPANY (CANADA) LIMITED

A new company that came to Woodstock, bringing an enviable reputation with it, was Gardner-Denver Company (Canada) Limited. Post-war Woodstock was creating a favourable impression on American industrialists anxious to expand into Canada.

In 1859 a Scottish immigrant, Robert W. Gardner, founded Gardner Governor Company, Quincy, Illinois, manufacturing his invention, the steam engine governor (a fly-ball governor to control steam engines).

The Gardner Governor Company played a prominent role in the exploration and founding of the Petroleum industry in Canada at Petrolia, Ontario, and Gardner pumps were used in the first oil boom of North America.

In 1927 Gardner Governor Company merged with Denver Rock Drill Manufacturing Company, forming Gardner-Denver.

In the past 108 years of operation Gardner-Denver Company has added many items to its product line. Today, this firm is in an enviable position throughout the world because it is a leader in the manufacture of heavy industrial equipment.

In 1950 Gardner-Denver Company started manufacturing operations in Canada for the purpose of assembling portable air compressors and mining and construction equipment for sales in Canada.

In 1956 the building formerly occupied by Bickle-Seagrave Limited was purchased. These premises, located on Highway #2 at the easterly section of the city, consist of 110,000 square feet and afford Gardner-Denver Co. (Canada) Limited the finest, most modern manufacturing facilities in Central Ontario. The company is situated on 85 acres which is ample property for future expansion.

The specific machines produced at Woodstock are: Compressors for diesel locomotives on tank and base-mounted compressors (air and water-cooled); several models of portable compressors in addition to special machines such as rock drills, feedlegs and stoppers for mining.

With the construction explosion across Canada, Gardner-Denver Company (Canada) Limited has furnished equipment for the following projects: St. Lawrence Seaway; Trans-Canada Pipeline; Adam Beck Dam, Niagara Falls, Ontario; the large Iron-Ore Deposits of Labrador, Quebec, and more recently, the British Columbia River Dam.

The Woodstock Division of Gardner-Denver Company (Canada) Limited employs approximately 150 people and the General Manager is David F. Quayle.

LA FRANCE TEXTILES CANADA LIMITED

A firm that has played an important part in Woodstock's growth is La France Textiles Canada Ltd.

In 1927 this firm was incorporated to produce cut pile plush fabrics for the upholstery trade and the original charter was taken out in the name of La France Plushes Limited. This operation was commenced in existing buildings previously occupied by Sterling Textiles on the corner of Dundas and Beale Streets and the Sturgis Baby Carriage Co. on the corner of Beale and Adelaide Streets.

Almost immediately, building was commenced to connect and expand these buildings. In 1929 the Dundas building was completely destroyed by fire in possibly the largest fire in Woodstock's history. It was replaced immediately, and on completion the Company had about 125,000 square feet of floor space.

While upholstery fabrics have remained the chief product, there has been a constant change in the styling of furniture which has resulted in a wide variety of fabrics being required, which employed the new synthetic fibres as they became available. Originally, the production consisted entirely of mohair plush and cotton jacquard

The disastrous fire which destroyed the La France Plushes plant on Dundas St. in 1929 left only a shell remaining of the original building. Freezing weather was a great hindrance to firefighters but resulted in some beauty being created and left in the fire's wake.

plushes but these were soon augmented by rayon plushes and friezes. From here the demand changed to employ a progression of fibres including rayon, acetate, nylon, polypropylene, dynel, etc.

Over the years there were many items added which were used for purposes other than upholstery, so that today, in addition to the furniture upholstery fabrics which include cotton and rayon velour, nylon frieze, nylon tapestries and blend homespuns, they also produce imitation fur fabrics, toy plush, paint roller fabrics and industrial fabrics.

From a payroll of about seventy persons in 1927, they have expanded to 325 persons. This includes the personnel in the Sales organization which consists of seven Branch Offices with stock across Canada from Quebec to Vancouver.

In a merger in the spring of 1966, Riegel Textile Corporation acquired the La France stock. La France retains its identity but it now operates as a division of Riegel Textile Corporation.

In the past year it has been necessary for them to expand beyond their original building and now have Iwer shuttleless looms and a carpet tufting machine in rented space in the Industrial Mall in Woodstock.

George Washington Jones, Town Crier. Mr. Jones was born in slavery in the Southern United States but spent the latter part of his long life in Woodstock where he was loved and respected by all who knew him. As Town Crier, Mr. Jones, or "George" to his friends, paraded along Dundas St. announcing coming events through a megaphone. Several Woodstonians serving in England during World War II reported hearing George's voice every Saturday announcing that week's regular dance. Woodstock businessmen were George's pallbearers and his grave may be found in the Baptist Cemetery.

Woodstock, one hundred and seventeen years ago, appeared like this to an artist perched on the steeple of the Old Knox Church. On the next few pages you will see how the City has changed and yet has managed to retain the beauty and traditions established during the nineteenth century. On page 187 — Woodstock was among the first cities in Canada to be photographed from the air. Here is the first, a photo taken in 1919 from an aircraft of the type shown, which was flown over the City many times in that year. On page 188 — Our main core area, from the air today, appears bustling, alive and prosperous. On page 189 — Our newly developed areas show intelligent planning with room to expand in the future. The homes are neat, well-spaced and have well-kept yards. Our City is blessed with many churches, parks, schools, play areas and convenient shopping com-

186

plexes. *On page 190 — Our City was developed first in the east end and in that area may still be seen reminders of the past 135 years. Old St. Pauls Church and its graveyard, in which lie many of our City's founders, sits proudly and peace-fully between York Knitting Mills Plant No. 2 (formerly Karn Piano and Organ Works and before that, a stage coach hotel) and old, quiet homes.*

WOODSTOCK, A CITY ON THE GO

As Canada enters its second century, Woodstock is riding on the crest of an industrial wave which could carry it to an enviable position. The present rate of industrial growth of the city is unsurpassed in its history. In 1966, the industrial growth was spurred on by the issuing of permits valued at $1,784,160, and the capital investments far exceed this amount.

The recent annexation of 600 acres, ideally suited for industry, at the eastern boundary, is providing space for the majority of new industries and new locations for older industries. Among the industries to move in here are Kelsey Hayes, Firestone, United Co-Op, while others such as Gardner Denver, Fisher Governor, Huddleston and Barney, Schell Industries and Unit Step continue to grow, as do Overland Express, Dr. Salisbury's and Holland Hitch, with others making plans to join them in the near future. The latest one to join is Alcan Homes, a division of Aluminum Co. of Canada. The industrial expansion does not stop here but is also to be seen in all industrial sections of the city. Standard Tube, Thomas Built Buses, Timberjack, Purina, King Metals and Canada Cement are all increasing their interests in the city.

All the progress is not industrial. There are great changes taking place at the Woodstock General Hospital where a $2 million building project is underway and when completed, the original home of the hospital will have disappeared and a four-storey east-west wing and two-storey north-south wing will provide 35 more beds plus a laboratory, physiotherapy and dietary facilities plus a boiler house. A new $508,000 nurses' residence is also planned which will accommodate 100 nurses. Provision has been made to increase it to twice the size when necessary. The present addition to the hospital is also designed for further expansion from its present 400-bed capacity.

The residential section of the city, while not as vigorous as it was a year or more ago, continues to grow at a steady pace with the trend being to town and apartment houses. Apartments are springing up in all sections of the city with a major project taking place in Hillside Heights subdivision overlooking Highway 401 in the southeast section of the city. One 30-unit apartment is completed and a 40-unit building is planned. More are also planned for the Lakeside subdivision overlooking Pittock Dam.

The completion of the Pittock Dam and conservation area will provide a handy recreation area for all who enjoy water sports and is a potential tourist attraction for years to come.

To accommodate the steady increase in population which reached 23,877 in 1966, shopping centres have started to replace the independent merchant. The largest of these to be established is on the site of the old Massey Harris plant.

Spiritual and education facilities have kept pace with progress and today few cities of its size can offer more to its residents. Scholastic achievements of its students are found in the numbers attending universities in neighbouring communities. The Separate Schools, which started with one school in the west end in 1900, had 113 students by 1913. It was forty years before a four-room school was erected in the east end. St. Rita's School was opened in 1953 with 73 students, which when combined with St. Mary's, made a total enrolment of 235.

The rapid growth of the city and, especially of the Catholic population, necessitated further expansion and in 1966 four rooms were added at St. Joseph's and two rooms at St. Patrick's. Now four schools are maintained by the Separate School Board with 951 students. The annual estimated expenditure is $271,885.00.

The question now asked is, "What makes Woodstock the city it is?" There are many answers, but the chief reason has been the faith industrialists have placed in the City.

THE BEGINNING . . .